0.1%

JOIN THE CLUB OF THE RICHEST, HEALTHIEST, HAPPIEST

SIMEON IVANOV

Edited by
ALLISTER THOMPSON

LIMITLESS ACADEMY LLC.

DEDICATION

To my mother, Rumyana, who taught me the art of gratitude, selflessness, and unconditional love.

To my father, Yanko, who taught me the art of bravery, honor, and drive always to make tomorrow better than yesterday.

To my brother, Dimitar, who has always been and always will be my best mentor and my best friend.

To my grandparents, Nedyalka, Dimitar, Todorka, and Stoycho, who dedicated their lives to raising me up and instilling the best values in me.

To my wife, Teodora, who opened my eyes and taught me how to be myself for the first time in my life.

I love you all with all my heart! Thank you!

ACKNOWLEDGMENTS

This book includes many of the most important lessons I've learned in my life. Hence, it's hard to say that it's my book. It's rather a book that came to life thanks to everyone who has impacted my journey. I want to express my deep appreciation to all members of my family, my friends, all my teachers, company team members, business partners, the countless mentors, coaches, and writers. I also want to say a huge thank-you to everyone who spent precious time reading my terrible first drafts and gave me invaluable ideas to make this book a much greater piece of work. A very special thank-you to my wife, without whom this book might not have existed at all. And a big thank-you to my brother, who "unsucked" the book on several occasions. Finally, I would like to acknowledge my editor, Allister Thompson, for the incredible work he did to make my amateurish style stand out as a quality piece of writing. Thank you all!

CONTENTS

STEP IV: THE METHOD

STEP V: THE RESTART

WINNING IS FOR YOU

"I'm such a loser. Just look at me. I'm so short and skinny. I want to be great at sports. But how can I play football and run as fast as the other guys with my asthma? How can I be good at basketball when I'm below the average height? I suck! I've tried everything, and I'm good at nothing!"

I'm nine years old, and that's just another regular day in my life. Another normal conversation going on in my head. Have you been there? I'm spending most of my time in that place, and it almost seems like it's the only world that exists for me. The world of self-minimization.

It's a typical Sunday, and we are in our flat on the twelfth floor of an old apartment building in Varna, Bulgaria. My mom has cooked our favorite meal for lunch: spaghetti with sugar. I will one day come to understand that my parents make this so often not because they believe it's a great meal but because it's the only thing we can afford. Who cares? It tastes great!

My older brother and I don't struggle with the fact that we are a bit on the poor side. Our parents are doing a great job of making sure we are taken care of. However, I'm in pain because I don't know who I am. I want to be good at something. I want to make my parents and my brother proud. I want to! But I can't!

Our home from 1988 until 2003

Mmm, the spaghetti tastes so delicious again! And things are about to get even better. The Formula 1 Grand Prix at the legendary track of Spa-Francorchamps is about to begin. If there is one thing I'm a fan of, that's Formula 1.

The race starts, and I can't take my eyes off the old TV screen. Mika Häkkinen and Michael Schumacher are fighting for the win, among other legendary racing drivers. My heart races as if it's me in those beautiful and at the same time scary machines.

I'd love to be a racing driver one day. What will it be like? To be a part of something bigger than yourself. To compete shoulder to shoulder with the best of the best. To live above mediocrity. To be a winner…

"Simeon! Simeon! Are you watching?" My dad brings me back to reality. I realize I've spent the last minutes daydreaming of being a professional racing driver … again. I must stop doing that to myself! I'll never be a racing driver. I can't even see across the room without my huge dioptric glasses. Yep, I'm short, skinny, and wear those funny-looking dioptric glasses. Classic!

I guess I'm just going to be a mediocre boy in a small city.

Six Years Later

I sit for the first time in a professional racing kart. The smell of burned, melting tires and racing fuel has always attracted me, but I never thought I'd be sitting in one of those fabulous machines. Not the regular rental kart, but a real, powerful, professional racing kart. And now is my chance.

The racing track is closed for an unofficial professional practice day, and I'm the lucky amateur who is at the right place at the right time. My father happens to know the father of a professional racing driver, and I get the surprising offer to give it a try. "Yes, please!"

Wow, this thing is fast! Scary fast. I can feel my body cutting through the air, and it's surreal. I'm shaking, but I push anyways, and I enter a new, amazing world that I will later learn is called the "flow state." It's a moment of pure joy where nothing but the present exists. No past, no future. Just now. Me and this beautiful piece of metal. Have you ever experienced anything like that? When hours go by and it feels like minutes. That's one of those moments.

I have no idea what the hell I'm doing, but it feels incredible. I think my heart is racing faster than the powerful one-cylinder engine that burns at over 20,000 RPM (revolutions per minute).

I'm living the dream and enjoying every moment. I'm the luckiest kid in the world right now. I can't believe it!

After a few mind-blowing laps, I stop at the pits and step out of the kart.

Everyone looks at me in silence. My father is there too. *What did I do wrong?* I'm asking myself ... silence again...

It turns out my first ever laps were faster than the pro's lap record on that track.

A new dream is born in my heart. I never knew I was any good at racing (or at anything else, for that matter). But now I want to be more than good. I want to be the best.

The game is ON!

Several months pass, it's midseason, and I'm ready for my first race in the Bulgarian National Championship. I get on the track, and I put on my shiny new helmet and racing gloves. Wow! What a feeling! I've only seen this on TV, and now I'm part of that world. I wear a slick red fireproof overall, just like Michael Schumacher. Wow! Just wow!

The first Free Practice is over, and I come to the pits excited to see the results. I look at the screens, and I start searching for my name from the top down. I look up, and then lower, and lower, and lower, and lower ... I'm last! And it's bad. My lap times are far behind the guy before me.

It turns out that the racing driver whose lap time I beat a few months earlier is the slowest in the whole National Championship. Well, not anymore ... *How can I be such an idiot?! What was I thinking? I'm never going to be successful in racing!*

I am so ashamed that I run away from the screens in hopes that nobody will ask me who I am and then check for my name on the monitors. I'm still taking off my helmet with my head down, and my parents join me.

I'll never forget what my dad said. "You're last. Did you see?"

...

My heart stops. My legs are weak. I want to run away. I feel my eyes fill with tears, and I turn away so that my parents don't see me crying. My whole body starts shaking with fear. That very familiar fear of not being enough. And even worse — not being enough for my parents.

When my dad asked me if I wanted to start racing a few months earlier, I knew he would spend our whole family's budget to make this a reality for me. To give me the chance to succeed for the first time in my life. My entire family would have to sacrifice everything for me.

Am I about to let them down one more time? Am I about to play the victim and the hurt game once again? This isn't about me anymore. It's about us. My parents didn't raise a loser! They deserve to see me happy!

I'm so angry! Angry at myself! Angry at my thoughts!

I'm not a loser. I can only lose if I quit! Just like I've always done in the past.

I spend the next thirty minutes away from everyone, thinking about what just happened. And I realize I have a choice to make. Either I quit now and never race again, or I commit to something.

I can't be a failure. I can't play small for the rest of my life.

And that very moment I promise myself:

I will never have to hear those words again! I will never be last! And I will leave my heart on the racing track to become a winner!

Something has changed. I'm not sure what, but everything appears different to me now. I feel awake. The pain is gone. The stress is gone. There's only this burning drive. This screaming new belief that I can make it.

So guess what I do during the off-season period? I wake up before sunrise, and I practice. While other kids are playing video games, I'm at the gym, four hours a day. While other kids are out having fun with friends, I'm at the racing track with my racing coach. Freezing winter winds are piercing through our clothes, but we are still there, timing the milliseconds. Lap, after lap, after lap, after lap. And I push. I push to the limit. I drive until I can't feel my hands and neck anymore.

"Simeon, when will you become a champion?" one of my classmates asks me at a gathering.

"Never. Not until I'm racing." One of my competitors breaks into the conversation before I get the chance to answer.

This guy is a seven-time national champion with tons of international experience. But I don't care about his experience. I don't even bother to answer. I don't care that my friends keep on telling me I have no chance against those guys. It hurts, but that won't stop me. I know what my commitment is, and I know what I need to do. I'm never going to hear those words again. It's time for me to be a winner.

And when my first full racing season starts, it's time to turn this commitment into a reality. Only I have now raised the bar, and I decide not just to go for the national title but also for the FIA South-East European Championship title.

In the first race of the FIA Championship, I crash, and I get a DNF (Did Not Finish). Things don't look too promising.

In the next race, I finish second. Back in the fight for the title.

The third race is in my country, in my home city of Varna. The same track where less than a year ago I tested a professional racing kart for the first time. And I'm kicking ass. I'm faster than everyone during the Free Practice. It seems like this could be my first win. I can see myself celebrating and spraying champagne from the highest step of the podium. What an exciting vision …

And then, during the second Free Practice, I come out of a corner at a speed of around 120km/h (75mph), and my tires touch the tires of a competitor. Before I realize what's happening, my kart launches high into the air…

Have you experienced one of those slow-motion moments when you are 100 percent present with the catastrophe that's about to happen?

This is going to hurt…

BHAAAM!!!

I hear a sharp cracking in my ears, and my heart stops! I can't breathe!

Ten minutes later, my parents take me to the nearest hospital.

"You have three broken ribs, my friend. Take these pills, go home, don't move around much, and take some rest today. You'll have to come to see me tomorrow morning," says the doctor.

I'm shocked! "I'm not going home. I have to go back to the racing track…"

"Don't be silly! You can't even walk. You know you cannot race like that. Now take your pills and go get some rest," the doctor insists.

"It's okay. There will be many other races…" My mom and dad start trying to calm me down.

But I know there won't be many other races quite like that. If I quit now, I will have no chance to win the championship. I might not even finish in the top three. And that might be the end of my racing career. If I race, at least I'll keep my chances.

So I gather some courage to speak up. "I'm going back to the track. You are the doctor. You tell me what you can do so I can go back and race."

My mother's eyes fill with tears. My father looks in disbelief but decides to let me lead that conversation.

"That's your choice. I'm just telling you that you won't make it in such pain. And it's dangerous. What if..." The doctor keeps pushing.

"Just tell me what you can do!" I insist.

"Okay. Let me think ... I can put a needle down your spine, and you won't feel anything for a couple of hours. But you won't really be able to race like that."

"Are you serious!?" I'm now starting to shake even more.

"I can also give you a few very strong injection shots and several painkillers. That will make you dizzy, but at least you won't feel that much pain."

The image of having a needle down my spine somehow doesn't feel right, and I'm happy to hear the second option.

"Perfect. Let's do that!"

An hour later, I'm back on the track. Nobody outside my team knows anything about my injury. The event's official doctors won't let me race otherwise. The painkillers seem to be doing a decent job, and I don't feel so much pain. Until the first turn...

I almost crash when the piercing pain runs through my body from my toes to the tip of my head. It feels like a thousand blades are cutting through every cell, sending agonizing signals that build up in my brain to a burning point of explosion. I've never felt anything like it before. I can't help but scream my lungs out and start crying while at the same time trying to keep my machine on the track. I realize I can't really do more than a single lap, so I come back to the pits.

"I will skip Free Practice," I tell the team. "I can really save that pain for later."

The Qualification (to qualify for a starting position for the race) begins, and just when I think things can't get any worse than that, my engine breaks down in the very first lap on track…

You've got to be kidding me!

Since I didn't complete a single lap, I must start the race last on the grid.

Is that a sign? I feel like the whole world is against me today.

Have you felt like that before? Like the entire universe is telling you to give up. To quit. To finish "last."

I remember my first race and that very first practice. I remember my father's words. "You are last…" That is never going to happen again!

"You don't have to do that, you know. We are so proud of you, and everyone here knows you can win this race. What you did was more than enough. You don't need to prove anything to anyone," my dad says hours before the race starts.

I try to fake a smile and hide the pain but find no words to explain what I'm about to do.

He continues, "I see you have made your decision. So if you go out on that track, just promise me you'll have fun. Do we have a deal?"

"We have a deal! Thank you, Dad!"

My mom comes and gives me the gentlest and most loving hug ever with her eyes full of tears. She kisses me, wishes me luck, and lets me get ready for the race.

I feel that no matter what happens, I'm blessed to have that support from them in such a moment.

I start putting my racing overall on, and my coach stops me. We realize there's something wrong with my fireproof underwear. The thick white fabric of the shirt is soaked with blood. I pull it up, and we see that a large piece of my skin has come off right where my ribs cracked. There seems to be internal bleeding that is pushing through to the outside.

"Simeon, you don't have to do this," my coach says in a deeply concerned voice.

"Just don't tell anyone," I answer, and I zip my overall back on.

I put on my helmet and hear the engines starting before me. Chills rush all over my body. It feels as if my heart has moved from my chest to my neck, and I can hear its fast and unusually strong beat racing through the veins in my head. I'm scared to death!

I can clearly see all the drivers in front of me. I'm starting … last.

Thirty of the most painful minutes of my life are to follow. The red lights flash one after the other…

3 … 2 … 1…

The race is ON!

I cry and scream my lungs out at each right turn. The gravity forces make every cell, every organ, every bone almost three times heavier and fiercely push the left side of my body where the three broken ribs are. I wait for a straight piece of asphalt to take a breath, and then I hold and squeeze my whole body, hoping to make it through to the next turn. But behind all the pain, I am still perfectly aware of this powerful thought in my mind: *I'm out here to win!*

So I push. I do everything I can. The pain is savage, but I don't quit. I try to fight through the field of all drivers in front of me. I try to stay on track for the full length of the race.

I take a last, sharp, deep breath … and I cross the finish line under the waving checkered flag.

I can see the whole crowd going crazy on their feet.

I can't believe it!

I won!

I finished in first place!

Still in motion, on my way to the pits, I open my racing overall and pull out the Bulgarian flag. The white-green-red colors shine behind me, blowing in the wind.

I use the last drops of energy to reach the pit lane. I can feel my body is about to give up at any moment. I stop at the technical "park ferme," and the engine dies...

It's over...

I rest my head, still with the helmet on, down on the steering wheel, and I can't help but start crying. I can feel the warm blood streaming down the left side of my chest. But there is no more pain. There is only this extraordinary feeling — wow!

I must have stayed like that for at least a minute, because when I looked up, I saw dozens of people coming my way. My team, my parents, the race directors, and even some of my competitors ... their faces painted in disbelief. They all knew now. And all of them came to express their respect. I'd never felt like this before. I won!

A month later, I won the last race in Istanbul, Turkey. I became the first Bulgarian racing driver to win the FIA South-East European Championship. Not only that, but I did it in my first ever professional racing season.

I was standing on the highest step on that podium, looking at the Bulgarian flag waving above me. The Bulgarian anthem sounded on international soil. I was a winner. And life was never going to be the same again.

I still find it hard to believe what happened next.

I won another South-East European title. I became a national champion. I was twice given the "Best Driver of the Year" award in the two years I raced in Bulgaria. A year later I got a podium finish in the Winter Cup in Germany. The next season I raced in the prestigious Formula Renault 2.0, and by the end of the year, I was part of the World Series by Renault 3.5. I had reached a step below Formula 1 in a five-year career. I became one of the very few drivers in the world who has achieved such success in such a short period of time.

Oh, and I raced at the legendary Spa Francorchamps just ten years after I daydreamed about it.

I guess it doesn't matter how tall, how pretty, how smart, or even how talented you are. I guess it doesn't matter what people say, and especially those who try to pull you further away from your dreams. I guess what matters more is what you believe in and how much work you're willing to put in. I guess the size of your heart is a more accurate measurement of who you really are. Because even in pieces, that's what will bring you to the finish line.

You know, I haven't become a genius since I was nine years old, but I've learned one thing for sure: if the short, skinny kid with the big dioptric glasses could achieve something significant, so can you. Achievement is not for the "special" or "privileged," nor is the ability to live an extraordinary life. It's for us. The losers, the regulars, the average, the mediocre, whatever you've been called in your life. Winning is for you, my friend!

WAKE UP!

Did I start living the life of my dreams after my racing career picked up? Not really. I was nineteen years old and had zero dollars in my pockets. My parents were taking care of me and were spending all their money so that I could keep on racing. They were incredibly supportive, but that didn't prevent me from feeling like shit.

What kind of a champion are you if you aren't able to pay your own bills? I thought.

I was lying on my back in my small bedroom, staring at the white ceiling, thinking about how I wanted my life to continue. I turned right and looked at the shelves heavy with trophies — over twenty-five of them. I felt so grateful. This experience transformed my life. But deep inside, I knew things would start looking pretty ugly if I didn't change something soon.

Life … that was not it! Not if I put myself and my family at such financial risk by continuing with what was now just an expensive addiction.

I went to the living room, asked my parents to take a seat, and shared my decision. "I quit!"

That night, I cried until the sun came up. Have you ever felt like a big piece of you has been torn away? That's how I was feeling. Racing was all I knew up to that moment. It was my identity. It was the only thing that made me feel significant in any way. But there was something more there than the pain and the sadness. There was hope for something better.

Next day, I booked a ticket to London, and a month later I started a new journey — learning how to put money in those empty pockets.

After my studies at Kingston University, I moved back to Bulgaria. I was already twenty-two years old, but I couldn't afford to live away from my parents. I had to start making money fast! I remember thinking, *If I make lots of money, then my life will be perfect.*

So my brother and I went on and built our own company in the medical field. For years, we would work our asses off just to keep our heads above the water and be able to pay salaries to our small team. We would celebrate every hundred-dollar deal. But we had much bolder aspirations. We wanted to transform the industry. We wanted to set new rules to the game that was run by people twice our age.

Step by step, our company started growing and growing, eventually turning into this beast that was way beyond our wildest projections. In five years, our strong team of twenty-five members was hitting over $15m in annual sales. In a country with a population of seven million people, this was quite a huge deal by anyone's standards.

That's it! I've figured it out! Right?

Well, not really. The moment I came down from the "treadmill" after working 100+ hour weeks for years, when we finally paid all debts and gave ourselves our first serious paychecks, I looked back and realized my life sucked more than ever before.

I had the apartment I wanted. I could buy any car. I could fly business class to any exotic place in the world. But there was one thing I couldn't figure out how to do: I couldn't unsuck my life. I couldn't buy my way to happiness.

Thanks to my great ambition to make lots of money, my relationships with friends and family were broken. And so was my health. I realized I hadn't traveled or read a single book in years. I hadn't done anything else but worked, and worked, and worked.

Have you ever felt like you are climbing the wrong mountain? That's exactly how I felt. I thought that being successful and rich would bring me everything I wanted as a kid. Well, there it was — success. That's exactly how bad it could feel.

I realized I had been poor and happy as a kid. Then I'd pushed extremely hard to switch that around. And I was perfectly wealthy and miserable now. Life was not working for me. It was broken. So, at the age of twenty-six, I was officially "successful" and depressed. I didn't feel like a winner. I felt like I was "last." I had failed once again.

During those few months — I call them the "lost months of my life" — I didn't pick up the phone, didn't go out, didn't do any work. I didn't see any meaning in anything that I was doing anymore, since it was never leading to the life experience I was ultimately looking for. I was sleeping all day and hiding from the world, afraid even to answer a call. My team was counting on me, and I was hiding like a scared little kid. My family was freaking out.

Well, I guess that's not it either! Life's not just about making lots of money and achieving success.

"JUST READ THE BEGINNING"

One day I woke up and saw this book on top of the dining room table. It was half-covered with pizza boxes and paper napkins. I remembered my brother Dimitar pushing it into my hands a few weeks earlier when he came to visit me and tried to pull me out of my cave. He said something like, "Just read the beginning."

I pulled the book out, brushed the crumbs off, and looked at the cover. It was *The 7 Habits of Highly Effective People* by Stephen Covey. I was pessimistic, but I thought, *Why not? I'll read the beginning.*

By the time I finished the first chapter, I had to read the second one. And then the next one. And then the whole book. Stephen Covey taught me something very simple that day. Something so logical, so fundamental, which I didn't know at that moment in my life. It was the fact that we are the programmers of the games we play.

I felt like I'd just woken up from a very long sleep. Sleep that had probably been going on for the past fifteen years.

I started asking myself questions. What do I really want? What will make me happy? What will make my life exciting? Can I also be successful at the same time? Do I really need to compromise? Can't I have it all?

I realized I had become the extreme example of the popular local saying, "You can't make lots of money and be happy and healthy at the same time."

Couldn't I?

I spent the next few months reading book after book and diligently applying all the different techniques proposed by the authors. I consumed all possible content from Tim Ferriss, Tony Robbins, Dale Carnegie, Brendon Burchard, Brené Brown, and many others.

I can't explain how grateful I am for the transformation that these mentors brought to my life. My depression vanished in no time, and I was back on track, running my business better than ever before.

But there was more. Something was starting to open up for me. There was this sense of hope and excitement. Excitement about life. Something I had not felt for a very long time. I could feel there was another level in all of that. Another level in life that I could reach if only...

I was fired up! I got obsessed with figuring out how to make my life work at a much higher level. I wanted to find a simple guide, a system that would guarantee me the best of what life had to offer. No compromises. No mediocrity. I was going to find a way to create and sustain the best of everything that was important in my life: health, relationships, mission, emotions, finance, adventures. Success with fulfillment — at the same time.

So I started searching. I read a hundred of the best books and took some amazing online courses. I went to some of the top seminars. I studied and modeled the most influential leaders. I even went as far as going through a half-year program to get certified as a Neuro-Linguistic Programming Coach. I spent years of my life and a significant amount of my income in my search. The results were incredible.

But there was no answer to my question. There was no single book, online course, or seminar that would give me the kind of manual that I was looking for. Everything I was learning was amazing. But it wasn't complete for me. It wasn't sustainable enough by itself.

I remember attending an incredible event by Tony Robbins, a truly inspiring and valuable seminar with an even more amazing leader. Tony is one of my personal heroes and is responsible for much of my transformation. But something made a serious impression on me during the event. Many of the people I met were there for their second, third, even fourth time. And they were still trying to deal with the same issues that they'd entered with the first time. This reminded me of some of my friends who were quitting smoking for the twentieth time.

Some people come out of these events ready to create a sustainable change in their lives. But many come out all pumped up (they quit smoking, quit alcohol, go on a strict diet, buy a gym membership), only to go back to their old habits when life punches them in the face and the "high" of the event wears off.

I was starting to get extremely frustrated seeing how we, you and I, are wasting our potential and our lives. I was frustrated with the sadness and the lack of excitement in peoples' eyes. Dreams had become an endangered species. They were substituted by a half-trusted hope in a "someday" happiness that I knew would never come. People were searching for the ultimate answer in books, courses, and seminars, but the answer was not there.

I didn't want to live in such a world. I knew how bad it felt. And now I knew it didn't have to be this way. I knew there was a way for me and you to live healthy, happy, and exciting lives and be on our way to our most significant achievements. How did I know it was possible? I'll tell you how. People walked on the Moon in 1969 ... Do we need any more convincing of the scale of our capabilities?

So I continued my search.

One day, things just started clicking. I had accumulated awareness, experience, knowledge, tools, skills, and by mixing and experimenting with different strategies, I stumbled on what looked like a scrappy system that made achieving much bigger goals possible. And more importantly, it made me feel like I'm the happiest man on Earth every single day.

While testing this system, I realized it helped me get crystal clear on what I wanted from life and why I wanted it. It helped me strategically design and live my days and weeks the way I desired. It boosted my performance to levels I hadn't experienced before and allowed me to be my own coach by keeping myself accountable.

The system was bulletproof. No matter what I was going through, it was there to keep me on track and to make sure that I'm living the life I was dreaming of for so long. Best of all, it was so simple by design, a little kid could learn to use it and reap all the benefits.

I had found the answer to my question. And it was **YES**. You and I could have it all at the same time without compromise.

I decided to give my system a go. I would integrate it fully for a few months, and I would coach a few friends to do it together with me.

My brother and I, together with two of our best friends, started a secret mastermind group. Each day, we would share our performance from following our tailor-made systems. The results were … extraordinary.

To name a few:

All of us hit all-time sales records in our businesses by quite a large margin.

The wives of our friends called me to ask what the hell happened to their husbands — they were surprisingly happy and supportive.

We all found the time to read and expand our knowledge more than ever before.

All of us "magically" found time to sleep more and had much more energy.

We all experienced unmatched levels of happiness, confidence, and peace.

We all gained the courage to dream unreasonably big (by all standards) and to take significant steps toward those bold dreams.

The only one of us who smoked successfully stopped smoking.

We all started following healthy diets, which turned into healthy lifestyles.

Two of us went from fat bastards to getting a six-pack.

...and many more results.

I was shocked! And so was everybody else. The system worked! Not only did it completely transform each key area of our lives at the same time, but we could feel the massive difference if we went without the system for even a day. Simply put, life sucked when we didn't use it. That's how powerful it was. Best of all, whenever life punched any of us in the face, the system was there, ready to help us bounce back and keep going stronger than ever before.

I didn't look for this system when I started this journey. I just wanted to deal with my own depression. I had no idea I could create a life in which I wouldn't have to settle for mediocrity in any of the areas I valued. Back then, I didn't believe this was possible for anyone. Like many others, I thought that severe compromise was part of the game. "Yes, but I'm too busy. Yes, but I can't do it all at the same time." That was all a big fat lie! We never need to make such a compromise! We can have it all and achieve much more significant results in each area at the same time!

From this new place of knowledge, I started observing the world with different eyes. I could now see why some things worked and others didn't. I could see why some people succeeded while others didn't. I could see why we all find ourselves champions in one area of life but fail miserably in the overall game. And the answer was simple: a system.

Most professional and personal development books, courses, and seminars fail to deliver on their incredible lessons and content because of the lack of systems. They give you a list of fifty things you must do (often extremely ambitious), and they motivate you to go all-in. You get pumped for a few weeks/months, and you deliver until the motivation wears off. And then you stop, never to return. Until the next book, course, or seminar. It's an addiction that makes you go around in circles instead of constantly climbing toward the life you want to experience.

Setting extreme goals is amazing. It's even better to follow through on them. But what's best is to have a system that always keeps you on track. A system that is your own personal coach.

You see, living without a system is like going to the gym without a training program, only a million times more complicated. You do a little bit of this, a little bit of that, and in the end you get almost no results. Then you find an excuse to give up because "it's not working for you."

Living without a system is like running a large, complex business without computers. You are a great salesperson who closes a lot of deals but runs the company from the top of your head with no data and no software. In a few weeks, you're bankrupt and most likely hospitalized.

Living without a system is like living the way you are most

probably living right now: far from your potential. Far from achieving your bold dreams. Far from the levels of vibrancy, excitement, and happiness you could experience.

Life is a game. And this game is getting more and more complex the more freedom technological advancements are allowing us to experience. There are just way too many options and distractions to choose from. If you don't implement a bulletproof system to run your own life, you will never become a player in this game. The game will be playing you.

Now, you can certainly live like everybody else and get by just fine. You can approach life as a sprint, work hard for fifty years, and spend the last fifteen "enjoying it." Maybe you can. But that's just a great recipe for regret. Life is like a decathlon, and it must be played as such. It's multidimensional. We've forgotten about that somewhere along the way. If one piece of the puzzle is missing, the whole system is broken. I'm not talking about "getting by" here. I'm talking about living. Not existing.

If the top 1% are those people who are very successful at achieving financial abundance, there is only 0.1% who know how to do that while staying healthy and experiencing life to the fullest at the same time.

THE 0.1% CLUB

We've all seen people who are rich beyond measure but lead poor lives without much sense of joy and excitement because they are "serious entrepreneurs who need to take care of the important stuff."

We know that guy or girl with the expensive car that finds it physically challenging to step out of the driving seat because they are "too busy to exercise and eat healthy."

That's a big part of the "top 1%" that many of us are so jealous about ... I don't want to be a part of that group. Do you?

At the same time, we all know the ones who are all about healthy living or having fun but forget to take care of their money game. And when life happens (someone gets sick, kicked out of work, wants to start a business, or just wants to send their kids to a good university), they find themselves profoundly miserable and dive into regret mode.

We are all trying way too hard to become something we don't want. No matter where we are in life, we are blindly grinding to summit the wrong peak, not realizing there are better mountains to climb. We don't realize that we can start a journey that would actually make us both successful and fulfilled. Such is the journey to 0.1%.

Being a part of the 0.1% is not about being better than someone. It doesn't mean making more money than 99.9%. It means making more money than you'll ever need to live the life you dream of living. It means using the maximum potential you were given for experiencing happiness and perfect health. The members of the 0.1% Club don't compete with the rest. They compete with the best they could ever be. And that's by far the toughest, most meaningful competition you could ever face.

The 0.1% Club plays a whole different game. It's not about being financially free. It's not about being healthy. It's not about living a happy, exciting life. It's about all those things together. That's a whole new approach to life, my friend.

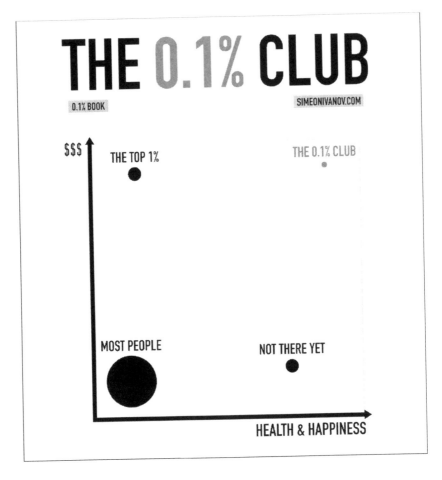

Obviously, much of the world has not figured out how to get to that place where everything that we value is taken great care of. Nor have the top 1% or those who only take care of their health and occasionally have some fun.

This doesn't mean that it's impossible to join the club of the 0.1%, to be financially free, healthy, and happy at the same time. It's not. In fact, it's simple. Not easy, but simple. Most people just lack the awareness that it's possible. Most people lack a system.

Wherever you are on that graph right now, it's time to realize that there is only one meaningful direction to aim at. And that direction is towards the upper right corner.

Let's expand this 0.1% together!

I'll share with you something very personal that I haven't shared with anyone before. If there's one thing I'm really scared of in life, it's regret. I'm terrified of it. I'm so afraid of this vision ... *I'm seventy years old, I look back and see all the things that could have been but never turned into a reality ... because of me.*

The 0.1% Club is all about living life with no regret. It's all about reaching the heights of your given potential in the fields that matter to you. You have no idea how much more happiness and excitement you can experience. You cannot even imagine how successful and fulfilled you can become. And you can feel vibrant and energetic throughout the whole journey.

Just stop for a second and ask yourself these questions. Who needs me to rise above the simple struggles of life? Who needs me to be financially free? Who needs me to be happy, energetic, and excited about life?

The challenge is most of us don't believe that success and fulfillment can coexist in harmony. Most of us believe that we can only have one or the other. And even worse, many believe they are not worthy of either of those. That is why the graph I just showed you looks so damn ugly.

But you know this isn't true. You know there is much more than what you currently experience. And I'll prove to you that it's possible. Hell, you'll prove to yourself that it's possible. And hey, even if you don't believe in this yet, doesn't it make sense to give yourself a chance for something better?

And even if you already are super successful, even if you are a part of the top 1% — **Don't let your dreams stay buried under the comfort of your current success!** And don't look for excuses for why you can't be, do, or have anything you want. We have full control over our present which is the building block of our future. And we have all the power to figure things out and create the life we want for ourselves and for the people we love.

Realize that the only enemy you are fighting in this game is the one inside your head. That little voice that says, "You can't make it; it's not for you; it's impossible." That little voice that made you afraid to fully be and express yourself. That same little voice that made you stop pursuing your dreams. That voice that made you present yourself to the world with your occupation, with your illnesses and disabilities, but not with your boldest aspirations.

That's us. We are the enemy. This voice has turned billions of people into experts at living sad, unfulfilling lives, and it has made us the best preachers of this false and nasty religion: mediocrity. And we preach it. We preach it good. And not because we are bad people, but just like that, by bad habit.

Life's not a game where you only get to pick whether you want excellent health, financial abundance, or an amazing family life. You can have it all. In fact, you *must* have it all. You must be both successful and fulfilled to win the game. And you can start living this life sooner than you have ever imagined.

I've spent the last three years developing this system from scratch. I've tweaked it a thousand times, I've lived it day and night. I've coached people around the world to use it.

Today, this system is my life. It's the one major thing that keeps me racing toward my dreams and makes every day of my journey feel like it's the best gift I've ever received. And more importantly, it touches the lives of everyone else around me as well.

This system has helped me reshape my life completely:

HEALTH: I got into the best health and energy state of my life. I went from getting sick almost every month to almost never (I haven't been sick for two years now). I went from "not being a morning person" to being THE morning person with an energy charge and mental sharpness that lasts me my full day, packed with activities.

RELATIONSHIPS: I intentionally started to create the most amazing relationships in my life. I rejuvenated my connection with family and friends and transformed it to a level I haven't experienced before. I met, fell in love with, and married the most amazing woman in the world. I learned how to connect on a much higher level with all the people in my professional life, which brought me greater satisfaction and greater results.

EMOTIONS: I went from being afraid of life to being excited about life. I learned how to control my emotional state and use it in a way that serves my present moment. In fact, things are starting to get a little out of hand because I'm excited to a point where I find it difficult to go to sleep. I once again wake up like when I was a little kid. I just have no patience for another amazing day to begin.

MISSION: I sold my business in Bulgaria and moved to Los Angeles, California. I uncovered the most exciting and meaningful mission I can serve in this world. I designed this mission in a way that sets me up for success. I did what I've been dreaming of doing since I was a kid but never had the guts to bring to an end: I wrote a book. I started generating three times greater results from a single hour of work. How's that for a change?

MONEY: I realized I'd messed up my financial future, even though my business was making a lot of money. Why? Because I was earning money, but I was not keeping any. So I started building my financial freedom and automated the whole process. This not only transformed what my financial future looks like but also transformed the past feeling of stress to a current feeling of calm and contentment.

TIME: I finally "found" the time to enjoy life and have fun. I travel more, experience different adventures, develop new skills, play the guitar, sing, practice sports, spend more time with the people I love. Oh, and I never spend a single hour that feels like "work" anymore.

Right now, you are holding this system in your hands. It's your invitation ticket to the 0.1% Club. I cannot be more excited for you. The transformation and results you'll be able to achieve after implementing it in your life ... I can't wait to hear about them, my friend.

I respect you immensely for your bravery to ask for more out of life. Be thrilled! There is more. Thank you for sharing this journey with me.

The promise of this book is straightforward. It will help you:
1) Achieve your highest potential for success in the professional field you wish to pursue;
2) Live every day with a great sense of vibrancy, excitement, and fulfillment.

Where other books tell you what you should be doing, this book will show you how to do it. Where other books tell you how to do it, this book will give you a bulletproof system to help you actually go and do it.

When you implement your system, when you do the work, you won't need to search for happiness anymore. It will be there for you. You also won't need to search for anyone's approval and respect. People will start searching for you.

Right now, it's your turn to make a commitment.

Do you want to join the 0.1% Club and start crushing the game of life? Do you want to be a champion, or are you okay with finishing last? I know what your choice is. I know because you are reading these lines. And you know it too.

Stop for a second and take a deep breath...

You can feel it in the tingling sensation racing toward your fingertips, can't you? You were born to be a winner. And it's time to make it happen.

Is it going to be tough? Oh, yes, it is. Are we going to feel like quitting? Sometimes, yes. But are we going to make it despite all the adversities? You are damn right we are.

There comes a moment in our lives when our dreams soar much higher than our biggest fears. And we feel ready to fight, no matter what stands in our way. We go for it full speed. And we crush it. We win.

This moment is now! You are ready!

Let's do it!

HOW TO USE THIS BOOK

For this book to bring the value it offers, you will have to read it in a particular way. If you don't follow the rules below, you will waste your time, and it will be as good as putting it aside right now.

Still here? Great!

I know you will be diligent. This is not about the book. This is about your life. Let me share with you the best way to use it in the rules below:

1) COVER TO COVER

Don't skip pages, and don't stop halfway through. This book is a system, and you cannot move to the last chapter without going through all previous ones. If you don't finish the book, you won't be able to start the system and experience the opportunities it makes possible for you.

2) TAKE NOTES

Open a new file/journal/note app or whatever you prefer using. It will be dedicated solely to this book and nothing else. Take notes of everything you find important, useful, or just interesting. We've all read enough books that we remember almost nothing about. Let's break this damaging habit today.

3) DON'T LIE TO YOURSELF
Whenever there's an exercise — do it. And do it exactly as assigned and before moving on with the book. Don't be an "I have to think about it" person. You don't get a six-pack by thinking about going to the gym. If you want the results, you must do the work. Remember all the times you thought about something and never did it? Don't repeat that same mistake here.

4) FOCUS – IT'S ABOUT YOUR LIFE
Read this book as if you are about to transform your whole life. Guess what? You are! Don't read it on the beach or on the train. Read it when you have at least a one-hour block of time, and you can focus. I'll do my best to cut off all unnecessary talk and include only what I know you need to make the shift you want in your life. Stay focused!

5) TWO FRIENDS
Ask two of your best friends to go through the process with you (share the book if you want). Do the exercises together and help each other along the way. You'll achieve much more when you share your journey with the people you care about (you know you do better when someone else is watching). What if you don't have two good friends who are willing to do that with you? Well then, buddy, let me be your friend, and you only have to find one more.

6) THE PROCESS

The book is divided into five main sections. Each section represents one of the five STEPS to building and implementing the system:

STEP I: THE WALL
STEP II: THE CHARACTER
STEP III: THE SKILLS
STEP IV: THE METHOD
STEP V: THE RESTART

All you need to do is follow the process. If at any time you feel overwhelmed, or you have a question, here's a way to get in touch with me or other readers in a private online environment.

Go to www.simeonivanov.com/p/book and sign up for the free online course, where we will be discussing all the topics from the book. I'll also be sharing valuable additional resources, updates, and info in this space.

I'm committed to you finishing this book and implementing the system in your life. You also need to make a promise to yourself to follow these rules. Integrity is the foundation of everything great.

For now, you don't need to know how and why this book works. All you need to know is that it has given me the life I've always dreamed of, and it has done the same for others. If you do the work, it will give you everything you want too. Just trust the process.

Let's move on, my friend! I know you are excited.

STEP I: THE WALL

THE POWER OF FREEDOM

We can easily forgive a child who is afraid of the dark; the real tragedy of life is when men are afraid of the light.

— Unknown

Whether we realize it or not, our subconscious is constantly working on ways to hold us back from building and living the life we want. It creates a thick wall of fears and limitations, keeping us in our small world of inaction, our comfort zone where nothing great can take roots and grow. The structure of this wall consists of six main elements:

- The Fakeness
- The Limited Liability
- The Drama
- The Fear

- The Failure
- The Chronic Misery

Without demolishing the wall, we will never be able to move on to the next STEP of the system. So this is exactly what we're going to do here.

Get ready to deal with your limitations and see what's waiting for you on the other side of the wall!

1

THE FAKENESS

You are a liar. No offense, my friend, but you are. I wasn't sure whether I wanted to start on such a positive note, but hey, this chapter is about honesty. But guess what? You're not alone. I'm a liar, and everybody else you know is a liar too.

I used to believe that I was the most honest person I knew. And more, I used to believe that I didn't lie to myself and others. But then I started questioning stuff. I went deep into analyzing everything I was doing, consciously or subconsciously, and how it was affecting my journey.

One of the most profound realizations from that little experiment was this: I am a liar. And a very good one. In fact, I was lying so much that my whole life was not working, even though I was an "honest" person based on everyone's standards.

We are so fake. We run around pretending all day long. We pretend that we are okay. We pretend that we can handle stuff. We pretend that we don't care. We pretend that we are confident. We pretend that we like each other. And then we go on pretending that we're not pretending. I like this last one the most.

I used to pretend about everything. I pretended that I was the best I could be in my relationships with my family, friends, my team at work. I pretended that I had no problems in my life and that my struggles were not a big deal. I pretended that I was not depressed. I even pretended that I was waking up on time. You've done that as well, haven't you? I pretended I was some sort of superhuman that was so much better than everybody else. I went so far in pretending that I even fooled myself into believing all these things. What an idiot, right? And yet so very human. This is what many of us do by default.

The result of my pretense? I lost track of reality. I lost power and sense of responsibility. How can you deal with the issues in your life, and how can you grow if you don't accept that there is an issue or an area for improvement in the first place? Well, you don't. And that explains much of the struggle our world is experiencing today.

We run around trying to look cool, pretending that we're not afraid of anything, not asking for advice or help, terminating our feelings, and shutting down our true voice. We kill the very things that we call human in ourselves. The result? We spend our lives surviving, not living. We spend our lives as prisoners of our own stupidity, prisoners of egos and "good looks." We live small, and we die even smaller.

Why do we do that? My honest answer to such questions usually is: "Who cares?" Knowing why wouldn't make the difference we are searching for. Actions will. But if we must analyze why, I'd say that we are just following what everybody else does. We are a society of egoistic, casual liars. We've become great at being followers. We've become experts at fitting in, at looking good, at creating and wearing our masks. And slowly but surely, we've walked away from our true selves as the years passed. It's just easy to be a liar in the short term. You can find an excuse not to take responsibility for anything.

But what if we were to change? What would life look like? How would we experience it? What would become possible?

Once I started transforming my fakeness into extreme honesty, I started experiencing a life I didn't know existed before. My relationships transformed to an entirely new level. I realized I didn't know who the people in my life really were. My truthfulness opened new opportunities for connecting on a much deeper level. A level with no bullshit. Just pure love and care. Pure joy. My productivity also went through the roof. There were no more made-up excuses and justifications. They vanished. All that was left was clarity — the best runway for action.

So here is the first big lesson: start with Extreme Honesty. This is one of the best gifts in your life — being able to stay true to your best self. Being able to see and name things for what they are and approach them from a place of clarity and responsibility.

Imagine a life where you are completely honest with yourself. Imagine how motivating it will be to accept your responsibilities but also your power to get stuff done and achieve results. Let's face it, we all know a hundred things we can do to start living better lives today. But we don't allow ourselves to do those things because of our fakeness habit.

What if you woke up tomorrow and didn't lie to yourself? You didn't say: "I can't do it." You didn't say: "I'm confused." And you didn't stop before you'd even started.

And what if you dropped all pretense in front of everyone who matters in your life? What if instead of saying: "Everything is great," you started saying: "I'm struggling, can you help me?" What if instead of saying: "Yes, that's fine," you started saying:

"No, I'm not okay with that. Here's how I feel about this and how I believe things can get better and why."

I can tell you exactly what's going to happen. Other than completely shocking everyone around you at first, you'll provide a great example of what authenticity really means. You will start experiencing life with a much greater sense of control, instead of giving up control to your lies. Not only will you start achieving much better results, but you will also be able to give and receive much more love and care from the people that matter. You'll start living a life full of new opportunities.

Extreme Honesty is not about telling people they are fat or ugly. That's extreme stupidity. Extreme Honesty is about using your authenticity to elevate yourself and the world.

So, after all the years of lying, how do you become authentic again? It's very simple. The mask you are now wearing will tell you that it's a long and painful process, but it isn't. Not if you do it right. You just need to start cleaning up some of your past moments of fakeness.

Yes, the first couple of actions might hurt a little. It's like trying to start an old car's engine after a cold winter night. Your mask will tell you that it's too cold, and you better keep things the way they are so you don't hurt yourself (hurt the mask). But that's not what your honest self wants. Your honest self that lives below all layers of past lies is ready to rise again. It's ready to take control. It has been there waiting for you to take action this whole time. And today is the day you do it. Today is the day you clean up the mess you created. Right now, you can begin opening the gates to a brighter future filled with much more power, success, and happiness.

How do you start? By sharing. Not on Facebook or Instagram, but with the people you care about the most. Call or meet with your parents, friend, partner, or coworker and have an honest conversation just like the one below. I call this little exercise **Extreme Honesty**.

(1) Greetings

Hey (friend), I wanted to share something very important with you.

(2) The Apology

I need to apologize for something.

(3) The Confession

I realized I've been fake with you/myself…

(4) The Truth

Explain when and how you were fake.

(5) The Damage

This has caused A and B.

(6) The Responsibility

I'm taking full responsibility for that.

(7) The Opportunity

I want you to know that starting now, I'm taking full control over my actions and will be completely honest with you/myself from now on. I will make it possible for us to be/have…

Here's an example from my own life (an actual conversation I had with my brother Dimitar).

"Hey, what's up? I wanted to share something important with you. I need to apologize. I realized that I've been fake in our relationship. I've been judging you for being negative toward me, and I never told you that. My hidden judgment has prevented us from having a more loving and trusting relationship. I'm very sorry for the way I've been with you. I'm taking full responsibility for what this has caused. I want you to know that starting now, I'm taking full control over my actions and will be completely honest with you. I will make it possible for us to have a trusting, loving relationship where we can openly share and support each other."

Notice the structure and order of this conversation. All the steps are critical to getting the results we are seeking. By following it, you make sure you don't fall back into judgment once again. Once you are done with what you planned on saying, you are done. Don't expect an answer, an apology, an explanation. You don't call to ask for anything. You call to apologize, take ownership, and state your plan for action. You do it because that will help you become an honest human being. The conversation doesn't have that much to do with the other person.

Even though I didn't expect anything in return, this conversation I had with Dimitar changed everything in our relationship. His reaction was invaluable in bringing us closer as brothers. He thanked me for being so honest and shared that he'd been doing the same toward me. Note that such truthful and warm conversations are extremely rare in a country where men are significantly better at sharing punches than feelings.

Imagine the consequences if we had not had this honest conversation. Two brothers not communicating authentically. The two owners of the company running around the office holding negative feelings toward each other. How would that have impacted the whole structure of the organization in the long term? How would it have affected our family?

Now, multiply this by all the people in your life. Yes, you are most probably doing that with everyone. Your friends, parents, partner, everyone. And worst of all — you are doing it with yourself.

How did I feel after this conversation? It felt like I finally dropped a massive rock I was carrying on my back. I then moved on with letting go of the rest of the weight by having these conversations with everyone — including myself. Suddenly, I could stand up straight again. It was a relief beyond my boldest expectations.

These conversations created a ripple effect in every area of my life. I was sharing my honest thoughts and feelings with the people I love, but in fact, I was healing myself. I was rewiring my brain from fakeness to Extreme Honesty. Slowly but surely, I grew into this new habit. Other than making me look somehow weird to the rest of the world, it helped me name everything that was happening in my life for what it is. It helped me take control.

Let me give you a simple, imaginary everyday scenario:

BEFORE EXTREME HONESTY
The situation: I'm sitting on the couch, watching *Game of Thrones*. My friend calls: "Hey, Simeon. What's up, man? What are you doing?"
Me: "Hey, (friend). Nothing new. I'm working on my book, as usual."

AFTER EXTREME HONESTY
The situation: I'm sitting on the couch, watching *Game of Thrones*. My friend calls: "Hey, Simeon. What's up, man? What are you doing?"
Me: "Hey, (friend). I'm being a lazy bastard. I'm sitting on the couch watching *Game of Thrones*, when instead I should be working on my book as I planned to do."

THE RESULT
In the BEFORE case, guess what I would always do? I'd keep on sitting on the couch, watching *Game of Thrones*. In the AFTER case, Extreme Honesty reminds me that I'm doing the wrong thing (the opposite of what I've planned). It reminds me that I'm acting

like a fool. This crappy feeling pushes my ass off the couch. I don't want someone to call again in five minutes, and I'll have to say the same thing. And for sure, I don't want to keep on watching *Game of Thrones* now that I feel like an idiot for not being honest with myself. Back to work!

You see, you can lie to the world all you want, but you can never really lie to yourself. Your subconscious is very well aware of what you are doing, and that's what makes lying so destructive. It adds layers of crap over what's real and important. It blinds you and keeps you away from taking the actions that will create a meaningful difference in your life. If we don't break the chain of lies and start practicing Extreme Honesty, we will never be able to see beyond the wall that separates us from the life we want to experience.

Your soul is like water. Stay fake and keep on poisoning the water with waste. Or start practicing Extreme Honesty and enjoy the purity of your inner world.

TAKE ACTION NOW

Have one conversation with a person who is important in your life, following the Extreme Honesty principles:

(1) Greetings
(2) The Apology
(3) The Confession
(4) The Truth
(5) The Damage
(6) The Responsibility
(7) The Opportunity

Hint: write down your part of the conversation before you make the call (unless you are meeting face to face). It'll help you stick to the point and avoid feelings dragging you back to your fake and judgmental being. Make sure you don't bring your bullshit excuses back. Stay honest.

Don't move on without doing this exercise. You promised yourself you'd follow the rules. It'll take you five minutes. Some of the best five minutes you've ever invested in your life. Start writing now, make this call, and I'll see you in a bit. You will love it!

Are you doing it already? I'm not kidding! Scientific studies have proven that if you don't do this exercise, somewhere a sweet, little baby kitten will get lost and possibly die. Also, if you don't like cats, they say it might actually be a dog. Either way, you don't want to be responsible for that, do you?

Okay, moving on.

This first part leads us to our next topic. And it's a huge one!

Let's continue with…

2

THE LIMITED LIABILITY

It was a late, cold night in San Francisco. He looked at his reflection in the mirror. He was going to have to sleep in this place again. A place he never imagined he would find himself in ... the subway toilet. Worst of all, his toddler son was there too, sleeping on a pile of toilet paper down on the dirty floor.

His life was broken. His wife had left him, he lost his home, he had no income, and no money in the bank.

"Why did this happen to me?" he asked himself repeatedly. But there was no good answer. He couldn't believe that just months ago he had so much. He had a good job that was paying decent money, he had his home, his wife, he had everything.

One night, back in the public toilet, he looked in the mirror once again and asked, "How did I get here?"

He could've attributed his struggles to bad luck or to a poor decision he made in the past. Or maybe to a lack of support from his wife and friends. He could've blamed God or the Universe, if he wanted to.

But this time, a clear answer emerged in his mind. An answer that would change everything.

"I drove here. I have something to do with all of what is happening," he said to himself. "And if I drove here, I sure can drive out of this place."

Struggling with homelessness while taking care of his son, this same man passed the Series 7 Exam, became a stockbroker, and got his life back on track. Several years later, he established his own company, which he ended up selling for a seven-figure sum. Today he is a world-renowned philanthropist, author, and motivational speaker.

The name of the man is Christopher Gardner. You might remember him as Will Smith in the great movie, *The Pursuit of Happyness.*

We are living in a world of Limited Liability Companies and Limited Liability Characters. You and I, we've been raised to believe that there are things for which we are responsible, and the rest is the responsibility of someone else. In fact, many have grown to believe that they are not responsible for anything at all.

You know what little kids say when they fight: "Yes, but he started it! It's his fault!" Well, unfortunately, it's not just kids. It's most of us.

"Yes, but I have more work than she does," said the team member who failed to submit his work on time.

"Because he also acts like a pig at home," said the wife who was asked why she called her husband an idiot.

"Because I wasn't born with a silver spoon in my mouth. I need to actually work," said the man who was asked why he never pursued his aspiration.

We run our lives and our businesses in Limited Liability mode, getting used to creating a ton of shit and not taking any responsibility for it. But guess what? This shit that we create ... that doesn't only affect the world around us. It affects us.

If you want to have any control whatsoever in this world and in your life, you'll need to start taking ownership of the events in your life. You'll need to become responsible. "Responsible for what?" someone might ask. Responsible for everything!

"But how come? Everything? What about the times when someone is obviously wrong? What about illnesses? What about tragedies I have absolutely no control over? Am I responsible for those things too?"

I know. We have a million excuses in the back of our minds. I have these too, and if I didn't use my system daily, they'd prevent me from taking effective action.

Of course, we are not always at fault. But guess what? Nobody cares! You don't believe me? Look around! Nobody gives a shit about who we think is to blame. Do you know why? Because it doesn't matter. It doesn't solve the problem. What matters is how we feel about the struggles in our lives and what we do about them.

We think that life is unfair. Life is *not* unfair. Life is just being life. And we must learn to deal with this.

From the first page of the book until now, I've purposefully used the word "shit" six times. I could've easily switched it to something that sounds smarter and less vulgar, but I didn't. Guess whose responsibility it was to focus on the message I was trying to convey instead of blaming me for my stupidity and my "shits"?

Just testing to see whether you are still awake, my friend.

You can go blame your buddy for not inviting you to his birthday. Act like an asshole to him. Make him feel bad. He deserves it. Right?

Blame the government for the economic crisis and for losing your job. Jerks! How could they do that to you? Bad, bad politicians!

Blame your parents for their lack of resources and your subsequent lack of a graduate degree. What were they thinking? Now you'll be a loser forever.

Blame your spouse for acting like crap the other day. She needs to be taught a lesson now. Cheat on her, maybe? I mean, why would she be such a pain in the ass all the time?

Blame traffic for being late for work. F*cking traffic, man! I know. Perhaps you should move to a smaller city.

You see, we can play these games all our lives. We can always find someone to blame for everything. We can say we are never responsible. Or we can say we are only responsible for this and that, and others should take care of the rest. But guess what? Well, nobody cares what we think or say. And no one will take care of any of the problems we have in our lives. And nobody should. Nobody but us. These are our problems. Everyone has their own.

You cannot solve a problem if you don't take full responsibility for it first. Chris Gardner could've continued sleeping in that toilet and put himself and his son through a lot of misery. But he realized he had something to do with everything that was happening.

In the same way, you can keep on living in the same crappy (mediocre at best) relationships, or instead, you can take full responsibility for the crap and start doing something about it. You can blame the president, your cat, or the position of the stars for the quality of your life, but the truth is you are the only one responsible and with power to do something about it. And even if you believe that you are not — nobody cares, my friend. So you might as well start believing that you are the only person responsible for everything.

Taking responsibility even in tragic and out-of-our-control moments doesn't have to hurt. You know why? Because we know life will happen. Bad things, like the loss of a loved one, illnesses, or tragedies will inevitably become part of most of our journeys.

And of course, we won't be responsible for all of that. But even then, we will be entirely responsible for what we do after the fact. And yet again, we can decide to play the blame game, or we can act like grownups and take full responsibility for our lives and our actions.

Google Nick Vujicic if you haven't heard of him yet and read his story. Watch some of his videos. Was he to blame for being born with no arms and legs? No. But was he responsible for playing the cards he was dealt in the best way possible? You are damn right he was. And boy, does he play them well! The guy is a hero who lives and experiences life better than most of us ever will.

Limited Liability is one of the ugliest traits of our society. It's a plague. What a difference it makes to see two people, one blaming everything and everyone and hiding behind foolish excuses, the other taking full responsibility and doing something about it now. The second one is truly an extraordinary human being.

So next time you feel the urge to hide away from responsibility, remember that you now run an Unlimited Liability Company as an **Unlimited Liability Character**. Don't let the quality of your life be determined by chance or other people's grace! Take control and become a great example for everyone else around you.

Instead of saying, "Yes, but…" or "Because he/she/it…" next time say, "I'm fully responsible for that. Here's what I'll do now."

Imagine if everybody started doing that from tomorrow … How different would the world look in twelve months?

TAKE ACTION NOW

(1) Make a list of three points. Each point is to represent a moment where you didn't take full responsibility in the past month.

(2) Call someone and share with them as many of the points as you wish. Let them know why you are taking full responsibility, what exactly you are going to do about it, and how you expect this to change your life.

Take five minutes and do it now before we move on. It's a simple exercise.

Are you ready? Great!

Now, let's move on to…

3

THE DRAMA

Our masks have another favorite tool: drama. We love drama. In fact, we love it so much that we let it run our lives.

I've seen people ruin their relationships, their careers, their health, their lives thanks to good old bullshit drama. But I've also seen people take back control and repair the damages that their own dramas created.

Dramas are those stories that our autopilot mode creates for us. And guess what? Our autopilot is nasty. It's managed by our deepest fears and weaknesses.

Not too long ago, I met a woman at a seminar in Dubai. Jenny (not her real name) was sixty-four years old, a proud woman, and it looked like everything in her life was taken great care of.

We started talking, and I asked her whether she thought something was missing in her life (not my regular conversation question, as you can imagine).

Jenny looked at me with the confidence of a top-level CEO and said, "Not really. My life is amazing."

But I felt that she was hiding something behind a very realistic-looking mask. I said, "Jenny, let me know what bothers you."

She softened a bit and went on to tell one of the most dramatic stories I've ever heard.

Jenny was nine years old, and she was waiting for the school bus by herself. It was a rainy day. She stood over a pond of water and saw herself in the reflection. At that moment, she heard an internal voice (translation — her autopilot) telling her how different she was from everybody else. The voice went on to explain how she was not understood by her family and how her parents and siblings were bringing her down with their negativity.

Twenty-one years later, Jenny divorced her husband. After the divorce, she finally did what she always felt was the right thing to do since her conversation with "the voice": she disconnected from her family.

"So you haven't spoken to them in over thirty years? Do you miss them?" I asked.

⁃ She was as cold as ice, as if nothing had happened. "I haven't spoken to them since. I don't really care about them. You know, it hurt when I left, but then all the feelings disappeared, and I really don't need them in my life," she said.

"Jenny, do you want to call them?" I asked.

"No, not really," she said, now sounding irritated.

"Are you afraid to call them?" I continued.

"No! ... Maybe ... I don't know. I guess. Yes, I'm afraid. I don't even know whether my mom is still alive. I don't even have any of their phone numbers..." she mumbled, followed by a long silence.

"Maybe that means I should call them?" she continued.

"Maybe. It's up to you," I said.

At that point, we parted ways because the event was about to continue.

Jenny is an excellent example of what we do in life. Something happens, and we automatically manufacture a dramatic story. Maybe on that day she wanted to speak to her mom, but her mom didn't pay attention to her because she was washing the dishes. Maybe her brother made fun of her and told her she was stupid. Maybe her dad beat her. None of those is a good thing. But that's as far as reality goes. On the other side, she made up a whole different movie. That drama looked something more like "My family doesn't love me!"

Let's see what happened next.

I was already a few hundred feet away when I heard a scream coming from the back.

"Simeon, wait, Simeon!"

It was Jenny. She was crying so hard that she couldn't breathe. I could see from far away something extremely powerful: I could see her as if I'd never met her before. Not the woman with the mask but the real Jenny.

"Simeon, I found him! I found him on Google. I typed in my brother's name, and I found his phone number. And, and..." She couldn't speak.

She hugged me and started crying even harder. I hugged her back, and I couldn't help but start crying as well.

"Jenny, tell me what happened? Is everything okay?" I tried to steer her back into talking.

"I called the number, and he picked up. I said, 'Hello, brother. It's me, Jenny. Your sister!' And, he ... he said ... he said — SHUT UP! ... He said — SHUT UP, I LOVE YOU! ... He said Mother is alive!"

Jenny went on and reconnected with her family after over thirty years. Her kids finally got to see her grandmother. Jenny was honest enough to tell me that until then, she only had three phone numbers in her iPhone, those of her two children and the number of her doctor. Well, now she had a few more. She had the most important contacts back in her life.

Even though Jenny's story is heartbreaking and may seem extreme, we have hundreds of our own dramas just like hers running our lives.

Let's have a look at some of the most popular dramas:

I'm not good enough / I'm not loveable / I can't do it / I've tried everything / I'm ugly / I'm stupid / They don't understand me / I don't care…

…all dramas.

Your teacher gave you a low score on an assignment (reality), and you decided that you're not good enough (drama).

Your first crush said "No" to your proposal (reality), and you decided that you are not loveable (drama).

You failed three times (reality), and you decided you can't do it (drama).

You tried four times (reality), and you decided you've tried everything (drama).

You realized you don't look very much like Brad Pitt or Angelina Jolie (reality), and you decided you're ugly (drama).

Your childhood friends laughed at you for making a mistake (reality), and you decided you're stupid (drama).

Your parents didn't agree with you (reality), and you decided they don't understand you (drama).

You didn't want to feel bad about your decision (reality), and you "decided" you don't care (drama).

Should I continue? I know this looks way too obvious to deserve a more in-depth explanation. It *is* obvious. But so what, my friend? What are we doing about it? In most cases, very little or nothing.

Most of our pain in life comes from our drama stories and not what is actually happening in our lives. I heard Tony Robbins speak about the movies we play on repeat. During one of his incredible events, "Unleash the Power Within," he said something that went like this:

"Do you have a favorite movie? And how many of you have watched that several times? Now, is there a movie you really hated? A movie that made you feel terrible. Raise your hands if you've watched that more than once…"

Eight thousand people sat still in silence. Everybody got the point. We don't go to the cinema to watch that terrible movie again. So why would all of us create our own drama movies and play them all day long our whole lives?

Once you've created this drama that you are stupid, how do you start behaving in your everyday life? How are you approaching situations, and how do they occur to you? Do you see challenges as opportunities, or do you see them as just another something to make you feel and look like an idiot?

When you play the drama that you are not loveable, how do you approach intimate relationships? Do you give your all and share your love with the person on the other side, or do you act like a protective, scared little fart? Do you find true love and happiness, or do you always end up finding what you are actually looking to find: the next disappointment?

The damages that our dramas create are apparent and very often massive. If you take all of them and sum up their total impact on your life, it's an undeniable fact that they've drastically minimized your potential. They make your everyday experience feel like crap. They make you feel weak and lacking confidence. They stop you from achieving your dreams and living your life the way you deserve.

Convinced enough that it's time to do something about our bullshit dramas? Let's do it!

Think of a moment in the past when a person you love hurt you by doing something. Maybe they judged you. Maybe they didn't do what you expected them to do. Maybe they hurt you physically. Just pick any real situation from your life. Note — don't pick an extremely painful case to begin with. Start small, and you'll build up later.

What was the reality of the situation? What happened, exactly? Write it down in one sentence on a piece of paper.

Example: "She said we should go to the gym more often."

Please, note that we're not going to go into your drama here. What did really happen? She said, he said, she did, he did. The reality. Not the drama.

I'll give you another one: "He said he wants me to leave him alone."

Okay, great. Did you write yours down? Let's continue.

What did you tell yourself that made the experience hurtful (your drama)? Write it down next to the other sentence.

Note, she didn't say, "You are fat and ugly." If that's what came to your mind when she said you should go to the gym more often, that's your drama. And he said he wanted you to leave him alone. He didn't say, "I never want to see you again." He also didn't say, "I hate you."

So what happened? That's your reality.

And what's that thing that you told yourself? That's your drama.

Guess who created that drama? Yes, it was you, my friend. Everything else apart from what really happened is just a drama that you made up.

Now, does that mean that she doesn't think you are fat and ugly? We don't know. There's no way to know until you ask. But chances are if she's with you, she probably thinks you are just fine.

What about him? Does it mean that he actually wants to see you? We don't know. Maybe he's busy now. Maybe he's stressed out. Maybe, maybe, maybe. But we don't know. Maybe even he doesn't know. But we make up that drama because we are afraid of uncertainty.

Why do we love drama so much? Why, in 99 percent of cases, do we go for the negative projection instead of creating a happy movie? Because our subconscious was designed to protect us from any possible harm. Evolution has prewired our brains as survival mechanisms. Our caveman ancestors needed to know if somebody didn't like them because this posed real-life threats. It was much safer (better chance for survival) to assume the negative. Today, this reaction is still programmed in our minds, even though whether somebody likes us or not is rarely a life-saving matter. The result? We can never be happy while constantly running from hurt. Because running from hurt is hurtful in the first place. And it's guaranteed hurt! What a stupid, vicious cycle!

You must understand the following: Happiness is for the brave. Success is for the brave. Do you want to spend your life running away from everything you desire? Or do you prefer to finally grow up and take control over your life? Think about all the opportunities you are missing out on because of your dramas. Stop taking pride in your misjudged abilities to read people's minds. You know you are wrong more than 50 percent of the time. And stop hiding in shame. Shame can only exist in darkness and secrecy but evaporates when you purposefully put it under the spotlight.

I'll share with you one of my experiences with bullshit dramas.

I was nine years old, and my math teacher asked me in front of the class, "Simeon, how much is 9 times 4? I want you to answer fast!"

I said it was 32. Remember, I wasn't the sharpest kid at school. I'll never forget her expression and her words. I felt like the devil was speaking to me through her.

"How can you be so stupid!? Give me your journal!" she shouted angrily, and she went on to give me the lowest mark possible because of my mistake.

This event was so powerful that I made up a sophisticated, multifaceted drama:

(1) I'm stupid. (So far, so good.)
(2) I suck at everything that includes numbers.

(3) If my parents learn about that, they'll kill me.

So I did what anybody in my position would do: I threw my journal in a trash bin, and I hid what happened until there was nowhere else to run (they found out a few months later).

My dramas haunted me for over a decade.

(1) I was crushing it at school, at university, at work, but I always had this belief that I was stupid. It was hard to convince myself otherwise. So what do stupid people do? They don't read books, right? Yep. So I didn't read any books unless I really had to for school until I was nearly twenty years old. Yikes!

(2) I always got the top grades in math, finance, accounting. But that's because I learned everything by heart. I never understood what I was doing with numbers, because I was "so bad" at it. Say whaaat?! And what do people bad with numbers avoid doing? They avoid dealing with numbers. They avoid investing. They avoid reading the company's financial reports. So that's what I did. I let my brother to do all those things and never looked at a single number. With time, this avoidance of all things numbers-related only reaffirmed my belief that I sucked. "My teacher must have been right."

(3) I've always striven to be a leader in any environment I found myself in. But guess what kind of a leader I became because of my drama? My parents were going to get super angry if I told them about my math failure, remember? So I decided I was not going to confront anyone about anything. I wasn't going to bring up difficult conversations, because I was afraid of making people upset or angry. How is that for a leadership skill?

It took me so long to realize that all the above was bullshit I had made up myself. My teacher wasn't to blame. I was. She did what she did. But these were my dramas.

Nobody can make you stupid. Nobody can make you bad with numbers. Nobody can make you sad and scared. Nobody but you. And it's not the reality that got you hurt and scared. It's the dramas that you made up afterward. And even when what happened is decades in the past, your dramas stick. They stick, and they show in every possible situation. And they ruin your life. They silently kill your potential.

It's time to kill all nasty dramas. Are you ready?

Take that same situation that you thought of earlier. Then follow the steps below:

STEP 1: Write down what happened (only what is real).
STEP 2: Write down the drama that you made up (only what you told yourself).
STEP 3: Write down the impact of your drama (all the negative consequences).
STEP 4: Write down the opportunities that will be available to you without your drama.
STEP 5: Share with a friend.

When we are not aware of them, dramas shape who we are in the world. They also shape how the world occurs to us. They prevent us from letting go of the past. They prevent us from being able to honestly forgive others and ourselves. They prevent us from clearing the path forward. Dramas become the masks that keep our true selves as prisoners in our own bodies and minds.

Today, you have a choice to make. You *do* something about it, or you continue *knowing* about it. I choose option number one every day of the year. I know you'll do the same, because your life matters.

Know that your dramas won't magically disappear in a single day. You've been feeding those beasts for quite some time. But once you become aware, you become Extremely Honest and take full responsibility, the dramas will start disappearing.

TAKE ACTION NOW

(1) Share one situation with two people in your life. Follow the five steps:

STEP 1: Write down what happened (only what is real).
STEP 2: Write down the drama that you made up (only what you told yourself).
STEP 3: Write down the impact of your drama (all the negative consequences).
STEP 4: Write down the opportunities that will be available to you without your drama.
STEP 5: Share with a friend.

(2) Keep bringing dramas up to the surface and repeat the exercise until you feel nothing is holding you back.

Ask your friends and family to help you with suggestions. They'll have a fresh perspective on all your "funny" ways of being. Just make sure you stick with what happened in reality and stop inventing any new dramas along the way.

It's time for the big one. Take a deep breath and get ready to deal with...

4

THE FEAR

A FEAR YOU CAN SEE – LITERALLY

Formula Renault. Monza racing track, Italy. Year 2007.

I'm overtaking Daniel Ricciardo (currently a Formula 1 racing driver), who is usually at the front of the pack. This is going to be a great lap for me! I come out of Curva Parabolica, and I'm off toward the fastest piece of asphalt in the Formula 1 race calendar: the Monza start-finish straight.

There is a sense of peace in me while I race that I cannot describe in words. Everything is moving so fast, but I can see it all so clearly. I must do a hundred things at once, but through the years of experience, my brain has learned to process information much faster.

I pull the lever and put the engine's transmission into sixth gear. The metal walls on both sides of the track create tunnel vision at such high speeds. All I need to concentrate on right now is the braking point for the first sharp turn.

The engine reaches its top revs at over 270km/h (167mph). I stay an inch away from the grass on the left side to get ready for the heavy braking. I smash the brake pedal as hard as I can with my left foot, and in a millisecond my brain switches from perfect focus to survival mode.

Instead of slowing down when hitting the brakes, the pressure bursts my rear left tire, and my machine is sent into an uncontrollable spin. There is nothing I can do, so I pull my hands close to my body to prevent breaking my wrists at impact...

BHAAAM!

I smash into the metal walls at over 200km/h (124mph). All of this happens in a matter of a few seconds, but it seems like an eternity to me. I can feel the pieces of metal and carbon fiber bouncing off my helmet as my vision becomes blurred by the smoke coming from the engine. I must get out of that car NOW!

The formula is a total wreck, but I'm fine. I'm taken back to the pits, and I get ready for the next practice session.

My team repairs the machine on time, and we are back on track. Something is wrong, though. It feels like I'm going faster than the session before, but my lap times are much slower. The practice is finished, and I sit together with the team to review the telemetry data.

The telemetry data shows everything that happens with the car and every move you make on the track. It gives you 100 percent visual representation of every detail: the percentage of throttle or brake you apply at any given moment, the rate at which you turn the steering wheel, the speed you keep at each part of the track, and much more (see example).

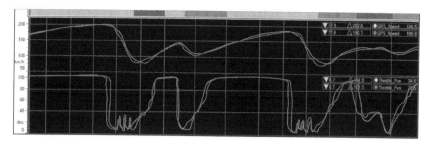

We sit with the laptop and compare my lap data with the previous practice to see what's wrong. And there it is. So clear, so obvious. I'm indeed faster in each part of the track, except one: the braking zone where I crashed during the first practice.

When we zoom in on the screen, we can clearly see on the line graph how I'm lifting the throttle, and I'm stepping on the brakes a few meters earlier compared with the last session. This tiny change is slowing my laps down by almost 0.500s, which in the world of track racing is a colossal difference. In our championship, it often meant the difference between being first and being fifteenth.

Guess what we call these 0.500s difference in such cases? Fear.

Now, there are two types of racing drivers, those who acknowledge the presence of fear and those who bullshit themselves that fear is not the problem (Fakeness). The latter will often find a million other excuses for why they are slower (Limited Liability), usually blaming the set-up of the car (Drama), but won't accept the fact that they were activating a subconscious brake (Fear).

The moment I see my weakness on the laptop's graph, I go to our team's office, lock myself in the room, and start working on what is holding me back. I work for about twenty minutes, using unique visualization practices that I've learned from the top experts in mental preparation — the same guys who coach F1 racing drivers.

I don't know what the result of this visualization will be. This is the first real-life scenario where I'll be able to use it.

The next session begins. I go on the track, and I break another personal lap record. We open the telemetry data on the laptop, and there is no sign of my subconscious fear. We can see that I was more precise, more aggressive, more consistent, and most importantly, faster at that first-turn braking zone.

A huge racing lesson learned. Later, I'll understand that this same lesson was one of the best life lessons I'll ever learn.

In formula racing, you can literally see your fear on the laptop screen. In everyday life, though, there is no telemetry data that will make it so obvious. We can't see our fears. We can't touch them. But they are there. And they prevent us from taking the right actions. They prevent us from stepping into the zone of growth and achievement. They prevent us from experiencing the happiness we deserve.

So what do we do? How do we approach this issue when we have no idea what's going on subconsciously?

The answer is we practice what I practiced on that racing track.

The result is we'll keep our foot off the mental brake that we push every time our subconscious smells fear. We'll make sure that we maintain a healthy level of courage and use our full potential whenever life presents us with a challenge.

NEW FEAR MINDSET

Fear is our greatest gift and our greatest curse. A gift because without it we won't be able to appreciate the joy and freedom in our lives. A curse because when out of control, it's the single biggest assassin of all life's meaning.

This goes to say that fear is not necessarily bad. It's only bad when we don't know how to deal with it and how to use it. And it's even worse when we don't acknowledge it — "Oh, no, I'm not afraid. I just don't like talking in front of many people." If you can't distinguish it, you can't work on it.

Fear is also the catalyst for anxiety, stress, and in some cases, depression. So we're looking to deal with all that in the next lines and create massive opportunities for a freer, more joyful and more prosperous life.

Before we start, let's all agree on something. Every great thing that we dream of is on the other side of fear. Period. That great relationship, financial freedom, the entrepreneurial challenge, asking for a raise at work, letting your voice be heard by the world ... everything great is there, behind this piece of the wall we call fear. And if you think you'll be able to coach yourself out of fear, you're wrong. It's not going anywhere. It's here to stay.

The great news is that we can learn how to use fear to our advantage. We can also learn how to tame it and prevent it from ruining our potential and our lives.

Before we get to work, I want to share with you a specific mindset related to fear. A mindset you can choose to develop further or shape to your needs that will make you much more effective later while doing the work.

So how about we start fearing less now? Let's begin with:

WHERE FEAR EXISTS

Even though we experience fear as something physical, it's not a tangible thing. You can't touch it, you can't see it. So where does fear exist? Where does it come from?

It comes from within us. We create it. Realizing that it's not external circumstances that create fear, but rather the meaning we give those circumstances, is the first step to fearing less.

Since we are the designers of the fears in our minds, we have the unique capability to generate some absurd scenarios. Do you remember that time you sat at home but felt like a lion was chasing you? Maybe you were fearing the upcoming bills and the decreasing amount of money in your bank account. Or perhaps you were just stressing out about the planned first date with this very hot girl/boy you were meeting that night. Either way, we've learned to enter survival mode in the wrong time and place for no good reason. And this unique capability is extremely damaging.

Seneca said almost two thousand years ago: "We suffer more often in imagination than in reality."

My subconscious fear on that racing track after the crash was attached to a powerful story that I made up: "If I crash again, my family will struggle with paying for the damages. If I crash again, I might not be so lucky as to come out unharmed the next time." Even though these sound like legitimate fears, I've chosen to be on that track, I've taken the risks associated with that, and such dramas and fears do nothing more but pull me back from performing at my best. Even more, they increase the possibility of such a catastrophic event actually turning into reality, since we tend to attract what we focus on.

So where does fear exist? **It exists only in our own minds.**

So far, so good. It sounds like we might be able to take control if it's not an outside force, right?

WHERE FEAR IS LOCATED IN TIME

What are you afraid of? Are you afraid of riding a bicycle while you are doing it? Are you afraid of driving your car while you are doing it? Are you afraid of speaking in public while you are doing it?

The answer is no. You are not afraid of the things you are doing right now. You are afraid of the possible consequences — the future.

Animals that are in the wild and are constantly exposed to life-threatening dangers seem to have mastered this problem. When they are being attacked, they switch into fight-or-flight mode; their biological system shuts off everything that is not needed and channels all the excess energy into one area: fighting back or running away. Once they are out of danger, the animals go back to their normal lives as if nothing had happened. And they hold no unnecessary stress until the next battle for survival.

With us humans, it's a little different. We can enter and stay in fear mode just because we heard a story about something we've never even experienced before. It's funny, but even our dogs, who pick up much of our energy and behaviors, learn to get stressed about a visit to the veterinarian before they have seen or smelled the doctor.

You can sit on your couch and be afraid of the upcoming bills next month. You can drive your car and be afraid of a potential crash. You can speak in public and be afraid of whether you'll be liked or understood.

But you are never afraid of what you are doing right now.

Fear is located in the future, but we carry it to our present.

If we learn to control our present emotional state (which we will), we might as well be able to control fear itself.

WHO FEARS

We tend to walk around in our everyday lives feeling somewhat special. But not in the good sense. We feel special because we believe that we are the only ones who are afraid of certain circumstances and other people. That's obviously extremely foolish, but it doesn't stop us from doing it.

The truth is, **everyone is afraid of you the same way you are afraid of everyone.** No exceptions. If you fear your boss, your wife, your husband, your parents, girlfriend, boyfriend, your buddy, that bully at school, whoever you fear, know that they fear you too.

Realizing that in itself will make you feel much more comfortable when you are around people the next time. Remind yourself of that when you enter the elevator with a person you've never met. Look at their eyes and notice what they're doing. Chances are they're counting the floors or checking their phone for no good reason, hoping this "agony" will end as soon as possible.

You are not special. Not in this way, at least. We are all afraid of life and of each other. When you know that, you'll gain powers you didn't possess before. It will make you less fearful and will put you in a position where you'll be able to help others feel much more comfortable with you and with their own lives as well.

With that mindset, it's time to dive into the fear work that will help eliminate hidden blocks that have been pulling you back from what you want to create.

THE FEAR LESS FORMULA

The Fear Less Formula is a simple system to unchain yourself from the fears that you know exist, but also from those that might be well settled in your subconscious without you realizing it. It includes two practices that are used for different situations in life.

Let's start with:

EVERYDAY FEAR

The first tool will help you deal with everyday fears like speaking in public, sales calls, difficult conversations, driving a car, flying, and other daily struggles we fear. That's the tool (with a few add-ons and tweaks from my side) that I used after my crash back in Monza.

A similar tool is often used in Neuro-Linguistic Programming (called Future Pacing) and is also implemented as daily practice by professional athletes around the world.

Let's dive right in.

Step 1: Find a comfortable, distraction-free environment, and take a seat with your back straight. Take ten deep breaths and then close your eyes. Don't rush it. Give yourself enough time to make sure you've settled in.

Step 2: Visualize yourself going through the day and facing the top two or three "scary" challenges you expect to encounter. While you visualize, see yourself from a first-person perspective. You are in your body, and you see from your own eyes, you hear the sounds, you feel the feelings. Make it as real as possible. You know what your usual emotional response to those challenges is. You might get shaky, your heart might start beating rapidly, you might get nervous. But not this time. This time you get to the challenge, and you experience an emotion of your choice. You feel confident, or motivated, or excited, instead of anxious and scared. You picture how you go through the challenge in the best possible way.

Step 3: Repeat Step 2 until you feel comfortable that this new emotion will be available to you when you face the challenge in real life.

Step 4: Finish your visualization by grounding yourself back to reality. You do this by focusing on the real sounds around you, on the feeling of your body touching the chair, or your feet touching the ground. Then you slowly open your eyes and take ten seconds to relax and stretch before you move on with your day.

That's it. It's as simple as that.

Since it might be difficult for you to follow the steps with your eyes closed at first, I'm going to give you an audio version of this exercise. You can access your free online course at www.simeonivanov.com/p/book. If you have already done that, go to www.simeonivanov.com/products/book-course and navigate to "The Wall," where you'll find the audio player and a download of the mp3 file (in case you want to have it with you at all times). This way, every time you want to practice the exercise, I'll guide you through the process. Just play the audio and focus on getting the result instead of memorizing the steps.

That's precisely what I did to recover from my crash. I visualized myself going through the whole track, picturing every possible detail, the colors of the curbs, the elevation of the asphalt, the sounds of the engine, the feeling of my hands on the steering wheel, everything. I was even sitting in a similar position as the one in the formula cockpit and was simulating the movements I would do if I were on track. Each lap I was doing in my head was the perfect lap. And I was experiencing a feeling of confidence. I was 100 percent focused and in the flow.

This exercise works for a single apparent reason: our brains are not equipped with the capability to fully distinguish our visualizations from actual reality. Thus, repeatedly visualizing an experience of a challenging situation and reacting to it in the best possible way to get the best possible outcome creates a habit without ever encountering the real situation in real life.

Sometimes it takes many days of practice to overcome an intense fear that has been settled in for years. But the more you do the exercise, the more you will get to experience the benefits.

Whenever you feel that you are experiencing fears that are pulling you back, start doing this early in the morning. Take five to ten minutes and equip yourself with the emotions and reactions you want to see yourself manifesting throughout the day. You have much more control over how you feel and how you express yourself than you have ever imagined.

MONUMENTAL FEAR

Some situations are more complex than our everyday fears, and our first tool is not well suited for them. There are cases where we need to take time to sit and analyze the situation and to evaluate potential risks and potential benefits of taking action. Sometimes our fears are pretty well grounded, and we must listen to them.

Such scenarios could include quitting your job and starting your own business, moving from one city/country to another, ending a relationship, etc.

Whenever you have such a decision hanging, realize that you must do something about it as soon as possible. The sooner you decide what you are going to do about it, the better. This takes into consideration that you've used this tool to analyze the situation and make an informed decision. If you do that, you'll be able to take it off your back and move on with your life. You'll also be able to feel happy about your decision. You've done the work before pulling the trigger.

I've used this tool to take many of the biggest and scariest decisions in my life that have led to my growth and much of the excitements I've experienced: quit racing; start a business; sell a business; move to the U.S.; spend a year writing a book. Many people use this tool from the top of their heads (they have this type of mindset), but I've seen more benefits in writing things down, because it helps with the analysis process.

A similar tool is also used by Tim Ferriss, who presented his version of it in a fantastic TED Talk called "Why You Should Define Your Fears Instead of Your Goals." Tim mentioned that he got inspired by stoicism and its teachings to create his practice of defining fears. He also shared that using this tool has helped him create some of the most significant changes in his life, including the experiences that led to writing his first, and one of my favorite books, *The 4-Hour Workweek*.

Take a look at this image before we move on with your own case. I've given you an idea of a typical example that many of us are either experiencing now or have experienced in the past: "Quit my job and start my own business."

WHAT I WANT IS TO ...		
Quit my job and start my own business.		
WHAT IS THE WORST THAT COULD HAPPEN?	HOW CAN I PREVENT IT FROM HAPPENING?	WHAT CAN I DO IF IT HAPPENED?
1 I can lose all my money, my house, my car.	Generate $20,000 safety net before quitting.	I can always go back to find another job.
2 ---	---	---
3 ---	---	---
BENEFITS IF I SUCCEED		
1 I'll be able to create financial freedom faster and work because I want to, not because I have to.		
2 ---		
3 ---		
COSTS IF I DON'T TRY		
1 I will live in regret for not giving this a chance.		
2 ---		
3 ---		
ACTION PLAN (schedule tasks in calendar)		TODAY'S DATE
1 Save $500 every month.		June 1st 2018
2 ---		DECIDE BY
3 ---		July 1st 2018
SHARE PLAN WITH		
James	Brendon	Jessica

You can download this spreadsheet from your free online course at www.simeonivanov.com/products/book-course (section "The Wall"). Sign up at www.simeonivanov.com/p/book if you haven't already. The file includes comments for each cell category with instructions on how to fill it in.

Here are the basic steps to analyzing the fears that are pulling you back and making an action plan that will pull you forward.

Step 1: What is it that you are trying to achieve but have doubts about and are pulled back by fears?

Step 2: What is the worst that could happen? Write down your top three fears related to this action.

Step 3: How can you prevent each of those three fears from turning into reality? How can you make it less likely (or not likely at all) that this will happen?

Step 4: What can you do, if it happened, to minimize the damage?

Step 5: What are the potential benefits if you succeeded?

Step 6: What are the potential costs if you didn't try?

Step 7: What are the top three actions you need to take to start making this a reality? Schedule them in your calendar and start.

Step 8: Fill in today's date. Then fill in your "Decide by" date. Think of "Decide by" as decide when to decide. It's crucial that you have a deadline for your decisions. This could be a date on which you'll decide when, exactly, you'll quit or not quit your job. If you have decided already, just put in the date on which you'll submit your resignation.

Step 9: With whom are you going to share your plan (don't pick the doubters)? Ask for feedback and ideas from people you trust and whose opinion in this particular area matters to you — basically, a person who's "been there" and has achieved the result you are seeking.

I have a friend who owned and managed a business valued at about five million dollars. He'd been building this business for most of his adult life. But he was miserable. He wanted out, but the firm was unsellable due to the nature of the organization. He wanted to build a new life. A better life. And his business was dragging this opportunity to deep, dark waters.

He'd been avoiding change out of fear for years. Some might ask, "What was he so afraid of if he was making so much money?" And I can tell you exactly what his main worst fear was, because he also used this same tool. What he feared the most was ending up broke. The same fear most of us have. So what was the result of his exercise?

He calculated his exact monthly expenses for the new life he wanted to build and started creating a safety net that would last his family for two years if he wasn't making any money at all (he was playing it safe). And what if he did end up broke anyway? The entrepreneur who was making so much from his own business wrote, "I can always find a job and be the best employee of a great company if everything else fails."

Guess what? He went for it, despite all the fears.

Why? Why would he want to do that? Why would he potentially take a step back, instead of staying where he is now? The answer is simple. After he did the exercise, he became very well aware that the risk was worth it. He knew he would "live with no regret" if he gave this opportunity a chance. And that was much more important to him than the extra money his current business was generating. He pointed some benefits such as, "My family will live a higher quality of life; I'll grow professionally and personally; I'll be happier." How much does it cost to be happier?

He scheduled his tasks from the action plan and got to work. His "Decide by" was six months ahead from the day he did the exercise. Long before that, he was already building his new business, a platform that is now on its way to revolutionizing a major industry. Something that might make him a billionaire. But what's more important is his eyes now sparkle like they never did before. And that, my friend, you can't buy with money.

Seneca wrote, "Most men are unwilling to live, and yet they do not know how to die."

Don Miguel Ruiz added, "Death is not the biggest fear we have; our biggest fear is taking the risk to be alive — the risk to be alive and express what we really are. Just being ourselves is the biggest fear of humans."

Don't be most men. Don't let your fears make you unwilling to live. Don't let your fears stop you from giving a chance to your boldest aspirations. Yes, be logical. Be smart. But don't forget to be brave. If anyone has done it before, you can do it too. If no one has done it before, well, my friend, maybe you can be the first one. Trust in your capability to figure things out! Your life is always worth the risk.

It's not about being fearless. It's about being fearful and taking action anyway. That's called courage. That's called living.

TAKE ACTION NOW

(1) Set up an alarm for tomorrow morning and practice your Everyday Fear visualization technique. If you want me to guide you through the process, go to www.simeonivanov.com/products/book-course and use the audio I created for you.

(2) Download the file at www.simeonivanov.com/products/book-course and analyze your most important Monumental Fear. Follow the steps as described. When you are done, take action or make it clear that this is something you won't pursue due to the potential irreversible damages. But make sure you become aware of why you want to do or not do certain things in your life and be happy with your decisions. Play the game! It's your game. Don't be an observer!

You are now one of the very few people who know how to fear less. So where do we go from here? What's our next best move?

Let's deal with…

5

THE FAILURE

"What if you fail?" my parents asked me.

We were sitting at the dining table at our home in Sofia. I asked them to have this dinner so I could share with them the important news. I told them that I'd decided to sell my share of the business and move abroad to pursue a new mission.

"I cannot fail. I never have. You see, every challenge I've experienced in my life has been nothing but a stepping stone for the next, bigger challenge. Every time I lost a race, I learned how to get faster in the next one. Every time I didn't get an A at school, I learned from my mistakes and got better for the following assignment. Every time I didn't win a client, I improved, and our company got stronger. But I've never failed. And I won't fail now either."

That was all they needed to hear to be able to let go of their fears. They knew I was right. They supported me throughout the whole journey, and they've seen everything with their own eyes. In fact, they were the very people who taught me that. And thanks to them, I've never failed.

Failure is a broken concept. When you go to Google and search for "meaning of failure," you'll get the following description:

noun: failure / Lack of success. / An unsuccessful person, enterprise, or thing.

What exactly is an unsuccessful person? Who decides what the metric for success is? Is it X amount of money in the bank? Is it the new Tesla Model S? Or a house with a swimming pool? How do you know when you've been successful or you've ended up being a failure?

You see, people are so afraid to live their lives because they are so afraid to fail. We are afraid to let go of our "secure" lifestyle (which often ends up being not so secure) because we know that the road ahead is associated with the possibility of failure. So we stay. We stay for years and sometimes even for the duration of our whole lives.

What we don't understand is that failure is not a bad word. Failure is not "lack of success." Sorry, Google, you are wrong! **Failure is a stepping stone for success. And the only way to fail our goals and our dreams is not to fail at all.** The process is straightforward, and it looks like this:

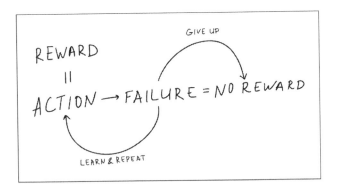

Or the even more popular example:

$$NO\ ACTION = NO\ FAILURE = NO\ REWARD$$

That explains the phenomenon everyone talks about: "the rich get richer, and the poor get poorer." Fear of failure is just like fear of investing. "Yes, but investing in a business or investing for retirement is risky. I might lose my money!" Thank you for letting us know, Sherlock! But have you made the following calculation too? If you never invest in a business or for retirement, you will most likely spend all your money on cars, houses, a new watch, an extra pair of jeans or sneakers. The moment you bought those things, you lost all that money, with a 0 percent chance of making a single dollar. It's a 100 percent chance of failure. If you don't go for the risk, if you don't take the possibility of failing at doing what's right, you are failing by default. Congrats!

In fact, the bigger and the more meaningful failures you are willing to go through, the bigger rewards you can aim for. In *The Everything Store: Jeff Bezos and the Age of Amazon* by Brad Stone, Jeff Bezos shared his opinion of what made the biggest difference between Amazon and its competitors: "They (the competitors) prefer to be close-followers rather than inventors, because it's safer."

Amazon has failed bigger, faster, and more than any other company in the field. Its failures and the lessons learned from them have made it one of the most successful and influential organizations in the modern world.

Failure is natural. That's how we learn to walk. We try a thousand times, we fall down (we fail), we try standing up, using our arms, our legs, our heads to get into balance. In a few months, we are ready for our first steps, but we've also strengthened our whole body throughout the journey.

When reporters asked Thomas Edison, "How did it feel to fail one thousand times?" after his attempts to create the modern light bulb, he replied, "I haven't failed. I've just found a thousand ways that won't work."

To be afraid of failure is to be afraid of living. We all fail whenever we try to learn or do something new. We all fail in our attempts to grow as human beings.

This feeling of you failing, that's nothing but a great call to action. This negative emotion generated by the understanding that you might not get what you want, that's your catalyst for your personally designed success. Without failure, we'd all be lazy bastards, sitting on the couch, watching YouTube videos all day.

I've put failure separate from fear in this book for one simple reason: there's nothing to be afraid of. Fear of failure must not exist in our world. We've just been stupid enough to give it the wrong meaning. Because the dictionary says it's bad. Because the media shows us all those sugar-coated success stories without any hint of struggle or failure. Because social media is full of our shiny, filtered, and censored images and videos. Because schools still make kids feel like complete idiots for failing at something. Because our peers are also afraid, so we think it's an excellent way to fit in. And last but not least, because our parents want to protect us — they've been biologically wired to do so.

In a perfect world, we must be afraid of failure as much as we are afraid of urinating. Both are necessary steps to leading a healthy, exciting life. You know, there is no way to guarantee that you will ever achieve great things or be the best at anything. But you can live with the guarantee that you can always give your best. And that's more than good enough. That's excellent.

So ... what do we do now? Do we take responsibility or blame the world for its wrongdoing on the topic of failure?

I knew you'd say that! We'll take full responsibility, and we'll start doing something about it now.

TAKE ACTION NOW

(1) Write down three actions you've been avoiding because of fear of failure (things you really want to do). Pick the small ones first.

(2) Write down the answer to the following question: What's the worst thing that could happen if I took action now?

(3) If the answer doesn't include anybody getting physically or mentally hurt — you know ... DO IT. Take the first small step. Experience this thrilling sense of freedom and power. My friend, you have what it takes!

Go on, do it now!
Are you ready? Amazing!
Now, let's move on and demolish the last brick of the wall...

6

THE CHRONIC MISERY

What needs to happen for you to experience happiness? Write down the top five things now. Is it a promotion at work? Is it a million dollars in the bank? A new car? A bigger house? A new relationship? A baby? A trip to an exotic location? What are those things you are waiting for that will make you happy? I'll tell you what some of mine were:

I'll be happy when I become a racing champion.
I'll be happy when I get accepted by a great university.
I'll be happy when I become financially independent.
I'll be happy when I sign a contract with this manufacturer.
I'll be happy when we make a million dollars.
I'll be happy when we make ten million dollars.
I'll be happy when I'm respected by my employees.
I'll be happy when I receive love from the people who matter in my life.
I'll be…

But I'm not. I'll be when ... but not now. Because the moment I got to that point when it all became a reality, guess what I always did? I immediately moved on to the next "when." And when it came to expecting someone else to make me happy — well, that's simply absurd. Other people have their own lives. Nobody owes us our happiness. Nobody but us.

So, what are your rules for happiness? Are you happy most of the time, or do you often find reasons to be upset, stressed-out, miserable?

Changing my rules for happiness was one of the most extraordinary experiences in my life. Simple yet so powerful.

Did you notice what was wrong with my rules for happiness? There were two major issues:

(1) They were all about the future and never about the present.

(2) They were all about what others needed to do or about outside circumstances, and never about what I could do now.

So here's what I did.

RULE #1:

I'll be happy when I put a minimum of nine strategic and focused hours of work every weekday toward achieving everything I want.

RULE #2:

I'll be happy when I give love and care to everyone who matters in my life.

The result of RULE #1? For the first time in my life, I was

experiencing happiness on a daily basis. Enjoying every part of the journey, not waiting for the destination. This boosted not only my happiness and health but also my productivity. Think about that. When do you perform better? When you are happy and excited or when you are sad and stressed-out?

The result of RULE #2? I could be happy whenever I wanted. Not whenever someone did something for me. I can always do something great for the people I love. I can always give them a call, share a kind word, help them with something, make a little surprise. And I love doing it. It makes me happy. And guess what else started happening? They started giving me more, without me expecting it.

You need to get rid of your neediness. Nobody enjoys it, not even you. People think they are entitled to receive. They are not willing to give without expecting anything in return. You be that person who is willing to be different. Be willing to give. Be willing to have full control over your happiness.

We believe that happiness is in things, events, and other people, and then we end up constantly disappointed by reality. So we keep on searching, asking for more and more, trying to find happiness where it can never be found.

The influential Indian yogi, Jaggi Vasudev (a.k.a. Sadhguru), shared in one of his public speeches, "If someone determines what should happen around you, you feel like a slave. But right now, somebody else is determining what should happen within you. Is this not slavery? Somebody can decide whether you are happy or unhappy. Is this not slavery?"

We live in a world plagued by chronic misery. We become slaves of our own choices and lack of awareness. Happiness is not a gift given to a few chosen ones. Happiness is a choice. It's in the everyday actions. It's in us.

Happiness is like a light switch. You are always one action away from turning it on (or off). It's your decision.

So what do you want your rules for happiness to look like? You can change them now. In fact, let me rephrase. You *must* change them now. Change them in a way that works best for you. Change them in a way that allows you to experience happiness daily. Not when you reach a milestone, not when someone else serves to your needs, but when you decide to. Not someday. Today!

TAKE ACTION NOW

(1) Make a list of your new rules for happiness. Make them 100 percent actionable.

(2) Share them with the people you love and help them design their own new rules for happiness.

(3) Bring this list with you and practice your new rules every day.

Congratulations, my friend! You've taken the first STEP. You've demolished the wall. This is essential for your system to work and deliver all the benefits you expect from it. Always remember that the brick walls are there to serve a specific purpose. Randy Pausch said that they are not there to keep us out, but rather to show us how badly we want it.

Let's see what's been hiding on the other side now.

Take some good rest, and let's move on to STEP II!

STEP II: THE CHARACTER

THE POWER OF SELF

"The only thing worse than being blind is having sight but no vision."

— Helen Keller

Once you've broken through the wall, you will be able to see the path forward. This will make it possible to shape the character through which you wish to experience the game of life. Without the limitations, you will be able to unveil your true values, create an inspiring life mission, and set up brave goals that will breathe new energy to your being and will provoke you to grow into your best self.

For the critics who will say, "Well, am I not who I am? Why would I need to pick a character?" Of course, you are who you are. But you can be a hundred different versions of yourself. You decide whether you'll be a lazy bastard or a person who dedicates his/her life to making a difference in this world. You decide whether you'll be a judgmental jerk or a person who purposefully designs and lives an exciting, fulfilled life. You are you. But you can, and you must pick which "you" you want to be. It's your choice. Nobody else's.

My friend, it's time to design your extraordinary character!

7

THE VALUES

A MATTER OF LIFE OR DEATH

It was a busy day at the office, as usual. I had just come out of a long meeting, and I was hoping to squeeze in thirty minutes to answer some calls before my next meeting.

Just as I sat in my chair, someone knocked on the door. It was a member of our sales team. From her expression I knew something terrible must have happened.

I asked her to take a seat and brief me on what was going on. She started talking nervously.

I was shocked. A young woman was dying in one of the hospitals we were partnering with (we supplied them with medical devices for complex interventions). What was worse, this woman was dying because her unborn baby needed to undergo surgery in the womb. And that surgery had to happen … NOW.

"So what's wrong? Why haven't they started the surgery?" I asked.

"The family doesn't have any money left, and the health fund won't cover the devices," she answered.

"You know what to do, right?" I asked.

"The devices are very expensive. Such surgery has never been performed before," she continued.

"I understand. But this is a matter of life or death. You can go ahead and do what's right."

She jumped out of her chair with a huge smile, even before I finished the last words of the sentence, and rushed out of the room to go and save another life (in this case, two lives). And she did. We did.

We were a medical distribution company. A FOR-profit company. But we had clear values. And one of those values was: "People's lives come before profit." We had an inspiring mission. And that mission included solving problems that no one else did. We weren't going to be like everybody else. We were going to walk the talk and be the organization that we dreamed of creating.

And we were. We saved those two precious lives that day, just like many others before and after that moment.

How long did I need to take this decision that day? The decision to put life before profit. It took less than a blink of an eye. Why? Because we decided who we were and what we stood for. And we lived these values day and night. Not just the management team. Everyone in the company did.

Did that make us poor? Did it make our company crash? Not really. It actually made us the biggest organization in the field five years from our launch. How? I believe a big part of it was because people trusted us. Manufacturers, partners, hospitals, patients.

And to be honest, there's no better feeling than choosing who you are and living that. When you go back home after a very tough day, you go to bed with a sense of clarity and fulfillment. "I've done what was right once again." How amazing it is to sleep with no sense of regret, knowing you are true to your values. Knowing you have done something that matters.

WHAT'S MORE IMPORTANT?

It's astonishing. We engage the full team, we hire consultants, we spend tens of thousands of dollars, we spend months ... to figure out the values of our companies. Then there are meetings to teach everyone about those values. Then there are videos, banners, and handbooks.

Yet 99 percent of the people in these organizations have spent zero time figuring out their own personal values.

I agree companies' values are in most cases extremely vague and ineffective (and they must not be). But what if we could approach this in a much more effective way? What if we can figure out what your deep, real, actionable values are?

STEPPING UP YOUR VALUES GAME

Have you ever felt amazing for no apparent reason? One of those moments when everything around you looked and felt perfect. Realize it or not, these are moments of full value alignment. And for a very good reason, they are extremely rare. But they don't have to be.

Unfortunately, we live in a world of continually deteriorating values. Values that lead to broken families, destructive decisions, sadness, pain, even death.

One proof of that is the fact that Western societies are experiencing an ever-increasing number of kids being born to single mothers, even though there are countless incentives for married couples. Data from the National Center for Children in Poverty illustrates some of the measurable consequences of that.

There is 5 percent of married family households who live below the poverty line, compared with almost 30 percent of single-parent households. What we still can't measure, and I believe would be an even scarier representation of the problems we are facing, is the effect this has on the future generations.

Almost every decision we make in life is dictated by our values. We either act to move toward perceived pleasure or away from perceived pain. And here's the problem. Our values don't come from within us. They come from other people. They come from our parents, from friends, TV, social media, schools, books, etc. From the moment we are born, the process of our domestication begins.

Bearing in mind the global trends, it is highly unlikely that you've been dealt the best set of cards to play with. What's more likely is that many of the cards in your hands may not be working for the game you want to play.

There are three huge benefits to exploring, choosing, and intentionally living your values every day:

1) The ability to create happiness and moments of fulfillment on demand, instead of just waiting for them to happen accidentally.

2) The ability to save a ton of time in decision-making and spare yourself some bad (potentially catastrophic) life choices.

3) The ability to create mental and physical space for what really matters in your life.

Before we are able to experience those benefits, we'll have to become aware of what's wrong with the current approach to the values of the surrounding world (including ours for now).

Societies around the world have become accustomed to

practicing "values" that are made of seriously damaging characteristics: externally oriented; non-actionable; non-controllable; socially hostile. If you don't believe me, you can go browse through some of the top Instagram accounts with tens and hundreds of millions of supporters. It's mind-blowing how porn-style images or images of a guy with a machine gun walking a goat on a leash can generate a raving fan base that is dying to be able to be in those influencers' shoes.

Most people (and I used to be one of them) with whom I've discussed this say, "Well, yeah. Of course, it's wrong. But it's funny." The problem is that the more we become okay with soft-porn photos being posted next to photos of little children, the more this becomes the norm. The result is that many children (and adults for that matter) believe that this is what being cool or great means. They believe that being famous is a must, and these are the best practices to get you there. They believe that you must have a fancy car and a house with a huge pool to be appreciated and to live a fulfilled life. They believe that you must be a jerk if you are to become successful. Why? Because that's what gets the most eyeballs, which then gets the most money.

Is it worth it? Does the "fun" compensate for the minimization of our life experience or the example we give to our families and the rest of the world? I don't think so, but I'll let you decide for yourself.

You see, exposing ourselves to socially hostile values leads to a chain reaction. It's like an invisible virus that spreads from one person to another, since we've been wired to subconsciously mirror the emotions and even the actions of the surrounding world.

Next thing we know, we've unwillingly and naively distorted the meaning of many of the good values we used to hold. And suddenly, we start perceiving pornography as "success" and cruelty as "fun." Do we want to let ourselves be deceived by such obvious disguises?

Consider what Seneca wrote in *Letters of a Stoic* two millennia ago: "I come home more greedy ... even more cruel and inhuman." He was talking about watching the gladiator games. "You should not copy the bad simply because they are many, nor should you hate the many because they are unlike you. Withdraw into yourself, as far as you can. Associate with those who will make a better man of you. Welcome those whom you yourself can improve. The process is mutual; for men learn while they teach."

We are responsible for setting up our value game in a way that serves the lifestyle we want to lead and the emotions we want to experience every day. A conscious, actionable value system that is in alignment with our true self is one of our most significant competitive advantages.

So, what do we need to do to make sure we don't get it wrong again? I already gave you a few examples of broken, distorted values. But what makes great values great?

A great value has the opposite characteristics of crappy values (obviously). It is:

1) Internally oriented – not focused on stuff or others but on self.

2) Actionable – you can do something about it now.

3) Controllable – it depends on you and not on the outside world.

4) Socially friendly – it doesn't cause harm to anything or anyone.

Some popular examples of great values are:
Hard work
Authenticity

Responsibility

Vulnerability

Humility

But even though these are great at their core, they are still bullshit values for one simple reason: they add no value. Why? Because they make great Instagram captions and bumper stickers, but they don't give the specific actionable meaning that we need to be able to live them. Their shallow nature allows for the creation of fake values and destructive behaviors like the examples given above.

When my brother and I started creating our company's values, we hired a professional firm to help us with the task. After several weeks, we realized we were going to end up with values that looked exactly like those of 99 percent of other companies — e.g., trustworthy, innovative, blah, blah, bullshit.

What does trustworthy mean to my team? That they must always say the truth, no matter what, or that they must always appear as trustworthy in front of the clients? What is a team member supposed to do to be acknowledged as trustworthy? Nobody has a clue!

We were shocked that even huge brand names and corporations had their Value Books looking exactly the same — as bullshitty as they could get. So we thanked our advisors for their service, threw everything we'd created by then in the trash, and started working from scratch by ourselves.

We came up (my brother mostly) with 27 Values that became the constitution of our company: our promise to our clients, partners, and colleagues. Based on these, we would also hire, reward, and fire whenever needed.

Here are a few examples from the 27 Values:

#1 The little things are the big things.
We strive for perfection in each detail of our work, from the design of our presentations to the way we package our products for clients. For each action, we ask ourselves, "How can this be done better?" And then we go and do it better the next time.

#2 We don't complain and make excuses, because we know it doesn't help.
We focus our efforts and actions on our circle of control (what depends on us).

#3 We learn from our mistakes.
We don't love them, but we see them as valuable lessons that help us grow. After each mistake, we always perform analysis and give suggestions for eliminating it in the future. To make a mistake and not learn from it is a luxury we cannot afford.

#4 A problem with a client = opportunity.
Each problem is an opportunity to do something extraordinary for our clients to reestablish our promise to them.

Do you see the difference? Other companies usually name those as follows:

#1 Attention to detail
#2 Responsibility
#3 Constant growth
#4 Customer-oriented

And that speaks absolutely nothing to anyone, other than the person who created these values (if he/she has any clue either).

What is a team member supposed to do with "Constant growth?" Grow a mustache?

You want to avoid making this same mistake when you design your Value Book. Remember, your values are not Instagram captions or company slogans.

How do we transform those bad boys: hard work; authenticity; responsibility? How do we make them usable and meaningful? Let me give you an example of how you could approach them:

#1 Hard work
Plan my whole week ahead and complete a minimum of nine deep, focused hours every weekday.

#2 Authenticity
Always be 100 percent honest with my spouse, my family, my friends. Share my feelings, my opinions, my thoughts.

#3 Responsibility
Make no excuses for anything. Take responsibility for everything that happens in my life, decide on an action plan, then act accordingly ASAP.

It's easy to know when you haven't lived up to your values when you put things so clearly.

You must know that great values are not easy. Having a value and holding true to it means you are willing to sacrifice something for it. When I say, "be honest with my spouse," it means I'm willing to go through tough conversations whenever necessary. When I say, "I always do what's right," it means I'm willing to sacrifice every business opportunity that contradicts with my chosen beliefs. That's a true value.

Mark Manson, the author of the amazing book, *The Subtle Art of Not Giving a F*ck*, wrote:

> "In the long run, completing a marathon makes us happier than eating a chocolate cake ... Starting a small business with friends while struggling to make ends meet makes us happier than buying a new computer. These activities are stressful, arduous, and often unpleasant. They also require withstanding problem after problem. Yet they are some of the most meaningful moments and joyous things we'll ever do ... This is why these values — pleasure, material success, always being right, staying positive — are poor ideals for a person's life. Some of the greatest moments of one's life are not pleasant, not successful, not known, and not positive."

If you haven't read Mark's masterpiece, I highly recommend you do (after you are done here).

THE VALUE BOOK

Extracting values might seem like a daunting process, but there's a simple way to approach this task that brings forward only what you genuinely care about in your life. Let's create your Value Book now!

Take your time and answer the following questions:

Question #1: What did you dream of becoming when you were a little kid? What were your reasons for wanting to become that?

Question #2: Remember a moment in your life that made you cry tears of happiness. What were you doing at that moment and why?

Question #3: Which types of behavior of another person have you always disliked? Why?

Question #4: Name two people you look up to. What are the qualities you value in these people?

Question #5: Remember a moment where you experienced feelings of deep gratefulness for someone. What happened, and what made you grateful?

Question #6: Remember a moment when you didn't back down on something you cared deeply about. What was that thing, and what did you value about it?

Question #7: If you had only three years to live, what would you do with the time you have left? Who are the people you will spend it with?

Question #8: If you were to die tomorrow, what would you regret the most? What are the things you would be most proud of?

Question #9: Look in the future, five years from now. Who do you want to have become? How do you want to be perceived by others? What is special about you and your behavior?

Question #10: Describe all the things you do and stress about on an average day that you shouldn't really care about. Why do you believe you must not care about those things?

The Value: Analyze your answer to each of the questions and summarize it into a single word or phrase that illustrates a value that is compliant with the characteristics: (1) Internally oriented; (2) Actionable; (3) Controllable; (4) Socially friendly.

The Action: For each value that you distinguished, write down a one- or two-sentence action statement. This statement must represent the exact ways in which you will be putting this value into practice on a regular basis. It will make it possible for you to know whether you are living up to your values or not.

You can go to www.simeonivanov.com/products/book-course and download a template of your Value Book from the section named "The Character." Otherwise, you can do this exercise in your notes.

Here's an example of the whole process.

Question #1: What did you dream of becoming when you were a little kid? What were the reasons you wanted to become that?

Answer #1: I dreamed of being a superhero. I wanted to be strong and have superpowers so I could help people in need.

The Value: Strength

The Action: I keep my body and mind as strong as I can. To do that, I follow my 0.1% system and try to improve every aspect of my life every day.

Question #2: Remember a moment in your life that made you cry tears of happiness. What were you doing at that moment and why?

Answer #2: I'd just learned that a kid we were trying to save will live and will recover fully.

The Value: Contribution

The Action: I've picked a cause and dedicate a set amount of resources to help children in need every month.

You see, strength and contribution mean nothing by themselves. But when you follow this strategy and you complete your Value Book, you'll build a set of inspiring, true, constructive, and actionable values that will bring your life to new heights.

Think about that for a moment. Do your everyday actions align with what you've just described yourself? Did you find anything unexpected about your answers? Do you truly live by these standards, or you often find yourself driving in the wrong direction?

It's very easy to live a life that does not align with our values when we haven't taken the time to analyze them and make them actionable. But now you've done that. So pat yourself on the back! You've done an amazing job, my friend!

Our lives, our experiences, our achievements are nothing more than a set of decisions and actions we take every single day. Every moment is an opportunity to shine. Every second is an opportunity to grow. Our values provide our characters with one of the essential tools needed for becoming a part of the 0.1% Club. They are the blueprint for our behaviors that can either make us or break us. They are the map without which we live in a world of darkness. Only when we equip ourselves with great values can we grow to become the great characters we envision.

TAKE ACTION NOW

(1) Create your Value Book now by following the steps above. Once again, the link for the template is www.simeonivanov.com/products/book-course, and you can sign up from www.simeonivanov.com/p/book if you haven't done so already.

(2) Set an alarm to repeat every day at lunchtime to remind you of your new actionable values.

(3) Print the completed Value Book sheet and put it in a place where you will see it every morning.

How do you feel, my friend? Are you ready for the next big challenge? The next chapter will blow your mind!

It's time to construct…

8

THE MISSION

WE DON'T FIGHT AGAINST COMPETITORS

My phone rang…

"Simeon, we have a fifteen-year-old kid with a ruptured aorta! Do you have a suitable size thoracic stent-graft in stock?"

My heart stopped. It was Professor Ivo Petrov, a good friend of mine who is one of the best interventional cardiologists in Bulgaria. I knew the answer straight away — it was no. I also knew no one else had these devices in Bulgaria. They were very expensive, and the health fund was not reimbursing them. So no distributor or hospital had any in stock.

The doctor was close to tears. I wasn't far off either. I told him I'd try to do something and asked him to wait for my call.

I called one of the regional managers of our partner manufacturer, a U.S. company with a European warehouse in Germany. She picked up right away.

"Anna, we have an emergency!" I went on to explain everything as fast as I could.

"I got you, Simeon. Let me call you back in five minutes," she replied and hung up.

I was stressed out. It was the first time we'd had such an emergency. I knew orders always took a few days to arrive, even when they were noted as urgent. But we didn't have a few days here. The boy would be gone by tomorrow. And it was already the end of the day ... I was hoping for a miracle.

A few minutes later, my phone rang…

"Simeon, one of our colleagues is on his way to the airport. He'll fly from Austria to Germany, pick up the stent-graft and then catch a plane to Bulgaria. I'll send you the details of his flight by email."

I couldn't believe it. A minute later, I opened my email, and I saw that their guy would arrive in several hours — at about 9:00 p.m.

I picked him up from the airport and drove as fast as I could to the hospital. As I ran through the narrow corridor toward the operating room, I saw the parents of the kid waiting outside. The mother was crying on her husband's shoulder. My heart was going to explode.

I rushed inside, where the physician's team was ready. The boy was lying on the table, unconscious, connected to all kinds of systems that were still managing to keep him alive. I handed the device to one of the nurses, and the intervention started.

So many people stayed late that night. The control room was packed with doctors, nurses, and people from the hospital's administration. I'd never seen anything like it before. I was there too, watching how the team performed the minimally invasive surgery.

It was quieter than usual. Everyone was holding their breath … hoping for the best.

An hour later, Professor Petrov turned away from the operating table and slowly walked out and into the control room. He started moving through the narrow, crowded corridor, looking straight into my eyes. He was crying.

It was only when he pulled his face mask off that I saw a huge smile on his face. He gave me a strong, brotherly hug with the words, "We did it!"

The boy was saved. A few days later he was back to his normal life.

The story got into the news. They were praising Professor Petrov and his team for the incredible procedure they performed and for saving the boy's life. They were praising our company for the support in making it all happen. But they didn't know that this miracle wouldn't be possible if not for someone else who got away unnoticed. Someone whose Mission was so inspiring, so pure, so powerful, that it made a gigantic organization (with over 12,000 employees) move as fast as a garage-based startup.

When I asked Anna Such, the regional manager, how much we needed to pay for the extra costs that their company accrued because of our request (the last-second flights and hotel, the time of their representative), her team said that there was nothing to pay for.

The founder of this company once said that they don't fight against their competitors. They fight against disease. And that's exactly what they did that day.

William Alfred "Bill" Cook died in 2011, but his Mission is still alive, saving lives all around the world. The name of the company is Cook Medical.

I believe that the two highest powers in our world are Love and

Mission. These are the two key ingredients that make up an exciting life filled with meaning.

It's painful for me to look at how people live their lives without a Mission. Some of us think that our intimate partners are responsible for bringing this missing sense of fulfillment to our lives, but that's simply not true. No wonder so many relationships end up in a disaster after years of broken expectations.

In January 2018, the most liked and shared article on LinkedIn was "Really – Always leave the office on time." This article was liked by over 260,000 people and shared by more than 70,000.

The author of the article shared such statements to support his advice: "A person who stays late at the office is not a hardworking person. Instead, he/she is a fool who does not know how to manage his time. He/She is a loser who does not have a personal or social life. He/She is inefficient and incompetent in his work."

And:

"You did not study hard or struggle in life to become a machine."

I'm not sure how to describe the feelings I experienced after I read this article. It was a mix of emotions, none of which was great. I couldn't believe that such a message was so widely spread and accepted in a professional environment like LinkedIn.

Do you think that if Professor Petrov and his team, Anna, or the manufacturer's representative who took four flights to bring the life-saving device were all following the advice above, that boy would be alive today? Are we all just fools who don't know how to manage our time? Have we messed up our work-life balance?

People have become so caged in their fears and their excuses. They don't believe that they can be great at both their Mission and their family lives. They believe they must make a severe compromise with one or the other (or with their health, hobbies, etc.). So they make career their enemy (some even make family the enemy) and thus never follow an inspiring Mission — living and experiencing half of their whole being.

The mindset is the enemy, and all the excuses about why we can't have something we want. Not our jobs, not our bosses, not our circumstances, our families, our lack of time. When you accept that there is a way to be great in both career and family, you'll take the time to sit down, strategize, and work until you find a way that fulfills this reality. When you keep on making the same excuses as everybody else around you, there's no change to be expected.

At the end of the day, it all boils down to the following: Do you want to be an A team player, or do you want to play in the B league? Or even worse — sit on the bench while others are playing. And that's more of a decision about who you are and who you want to become rather than about your work, your boss, and when to leave the office.

I doubt Thomas Edison came up with anything meaningful at quarter to five, while looking at his watch, getting ready to leave. Magic doesn't happen between nine and five. It just doesn't. Not if you don't commit to pouring your heart into the game you are playing. And if you are waiting for the clock to hit five to close the door from the outside ... well, maybe you are playing the wrong game, my friend.

Find this game where you'll never feel "forced" to work hard but will be inspired to do so! Not because of somebody else, but because of you and your Mission. Leave your heart on each field of play! Every day! The world doesn't need us to be the mediocre version of ourselves. It needs us to be the best we could possibly be.

People love talking about work-life balance. I don't see any balance in doing something that doesn't inspire you for eight to nine hours every day. I don't see balance in bringing this lack of fulfillment and half-heartedness back home to your beloved family.

It's a state of mind your spouse and kids didn't sign up for. Balance is not achieved by "always leaving the office on time." It is achieved by making sure that all important areas of your life are taken great care of (health, relationships, emotions, mission/career, finance, free time). If one of these is broken, the rest will suffer as well.

"Work-life balance" seems to have become the best excuse for many people not to take responsibility for their professional and personal growth. But this "balance" that all of us love to talk about is not something conceptual. It is achieved by strategic, focused, hard work. It doesn't come by default or when we say the magic words. That's why many of us are leading lives far from our potential for success and fulfillment — because we wait for balance to happen, and it never does. I've been there, and it sucks.

Most of us haven't taken a single hour of our lives to think about what work-life balance means to us. Needless to say, we put zero effort into planning about it, working for it, living it. Open your calendar and show me what your work-life balance looks like. In 99 percent of cases, it's not there — it's nowhere to be found.

What upsets me most is seeing the lack of belief in people who think that they can only have one or the other. People who think they will never be successful in following their Mission because they also have a family to take care of. That's only true if you want to believe it. You only need one example of a person who has it all — and there are many. We must not shy away from setting exciting goals. And those goals must include being great in both our professional and personal lives.

The author of the original article later commented that he didn't write these arguments himself. He mentioned that the source is the former prime minister of India, who is also a rocket scientist.

It turned out that the original seven points come from the eleventh president of India (2002–2007), Mr. A.P.J. Abdul

Kalam. The professor's achievements (there are many notable ones) and apparent care for the well-being of others are something that deserve great respect and also something that clearly illustrates that he, himself was not one to "always leave the office on time."

Who the source is, however, is less important compared with the interpretation of the president's words and the impact it had on the LinkedIn community.

If we are to see more successful and fulfilled people around us, we shouldn't blindly follow people's advice basing it on their CV, whether it says Founder, CEO, Prime Minister, President, or any other label that may sound important.

We must not use our families as an excuse not to take responsibility for our personal Mission in life. That's just wrong! It's easy to say, "I'm a family guy," and hide behind that story. But that's a made-up reason that lacks any amount of courage and integrity.

Balance is work hard, play hard. Not work average, live average.

I honor the fears and struggles we all experience. We are human. That's our nature. But we already know what giving up on our dreams feels like. I invite you to try to see what the opposite is like. There's nothing to lose. We'll all be gone someday anyway.

All the people who we look up to are there, on the field, playing the game. They are not any better than us. They just started and never quit. How long more are we going to stay on the bench to watch and comment? How long are we going to use our families, our circumstances, our gender, our age, as an excuse not to step in and get in the game?

We don't want our stone to say: "He/She was balanced ... and sad." I prefer mine (and yours) saying: "He/She played full out!"

Never listen to people who want to drag you down to their level of fearfulness! Prove them wrong and pull them up to your level of bravery!

YOU MIGHTS AS WELL TAKE A CHANCE

"So many of us chose our path out of fear disguised as practicality. My father could have been a great comedian, but he didn't believe that was possible for him. So he made a conservative choice and instead he got a job as an accountant. When I was twelve years old, he was let go from that safe job. Our family had to do whatever we could to survive. I learned many great lessons from my father, not the least of which is that you can fail at what you don't want, so you might as well take a chance on doing what you love."

— JIM CARREY

So many of us don't get that clear of an example as Jim Carrey did. So we stay on the "safe" path. We stay on the path we least desire. And we stay there until we are too old to remember what we actually wanted our lives to look like.

I understand the fear of change, my friend. I've given up my "identity" and the safeties of the present a few times already. It hurts, and it's scary. We believe it's dangerous, and it could be if we don't do it right. But there is a smart way to approach Mission design that can set you up for success and eliminate many of the potential dangers.

I respect the "follow your heart" approach. Our hearts often know better than our brains do. But there are exceptions to that model, and these exceptions include all the moments when we are not entirely aligned with our value system. This is when fear and limiting beliefs mess up the program of the heart, and we start getting false signals. Because of that, I prefer using systems and frameworks while still integrating the input of the heart at full speed.

There are a thousand quotes out there from well-respected scientists, philosophers, and entrepreneurs, all trying to convince us to "follow our dreams" or to "follow our bliss and never be afraid to jump into deep waters." While all that sounds great, as most fairy tales do, I know that for most people it simply doesn't work.

While media, books, movies always focus on that 1 percent who succeeded, nobody is really interested in that 99 percent who didn't. You and I are not here to read about positive thinking. We are here to strategically design a lifestyle that can actually turn into a reality. And to make it work, we need to figure out your Mission. We need to figure out your reason for being. The reason why you'll be waking up from tomorrow. We need to set you up for success.

DESIGNING YOUR MISSION

In a TED Talk and a series of books, the *National Geographic* writer and explorer Dan Buettner unveiled the world of the Blue Zones. Blue Zones (Okinawa, Japan; Sardinia, Italy; Nicoya, Costa Rica; Loma Linda, California) are those places in the world where, on average, people live the longest disability-free lives of all. According to thirty-year scientific research that Buettner's team studied, only about 10 percent of how long we live is dictated by our genes. The other 90 percent is dictated by our lifestyles.

The researchers established that one of the major factors for increasing life expectancy came from something quite unique: finding your purpose and living it. In fact, they shared that when done right, this can lead to an increase in lifespan of up to seven years. Yes, please!

One of the Blue Zones is situated on the island of Okinawa, Japan. What makes the Okinawans unique is that their vocabulary lacks a word with the meaning "retirement." Instead, they have a word that describes your entire life. And that word is *ikigai*. Ikigai can be roughly translated to "the reason for which you wake up in the morning." If you happen to go to Okinawa and ask the locals what their ikigai is, most people will have an answer straight away. What's more important is they'll be able to show you how they're living their ikigai every day.

This is what their simple system for finding their Mission looks like.

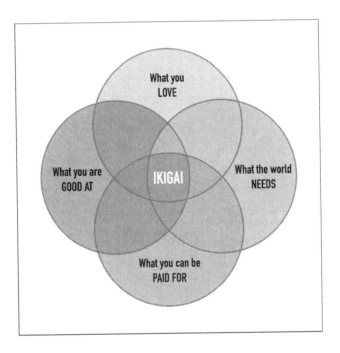

When I first saw this, I found it to be the most effective, meaningful, and powerful system in this field of study. It's a unique system that must have been long established in the Western world but for some reason it never was.

But after implementing it for myself and a few other people, I realized it was incomplete. It was much better than anything we've been taught until now, but it was missing a few critical pieces. Pieces that made it even more powerful.

So I redesigned it and implemented these two pieces to form what I call SMS (Simeon's Mission Set-up). Is that too narcissistic? Yep, I think it is. But I don't care.

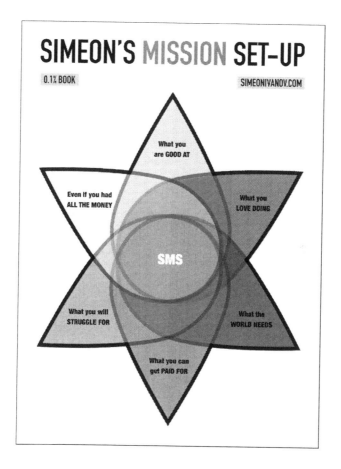

When we get to the tool in a bit, you'll realize that everything we'd learned about finding our Mission in the past is now far outdated and impractical. You'll feel this sense of excitement. New ideas will sparkle. Ideas that are meaningful, not just for your own sake, but for the world. Ideas that will bring a great sense of fulfillment and joy. Ideas that will set you up for success. Ideas that will help generate financial abundance for you and your family. Ideas that might even change the world.

I've seen so many examples of people and businesses that are getting this completely wrong. And they struggle. They set themselves up for failure. I'll give you an example.

I was driving through Koreatown, Los Angeles, and I was looking through the window and observing the local businesses. I went through one of the main streets, and something shocked me. There were five hairdressers, one after the other. Not two or three. Five!

Now, after the second shop, there were apparently three business owners who didn't do this exercise. Why? Because the world (this neighborhood) didn't need another hairdresser that was exactly the same as the other two, three, and four on that street. That's a recipe for failure and disappointment. And it's also a recipe for ruining other people's businesses. That's not a great Mission. That's called lack of awareness. I'll show you how to avoid that and set yourself up for success with fulfillment.

Are you ready to unveil your Mission?

The process is quite simple. First, get up from your seat and take ten deep breaths while jumping in place. I want you to forget about everything you are now, about what your job or business is. I want you to have a clear mind to get the best out of this exercise. Stand up and do it now, my friend. I'll wait.

Are you ready? Let's move on!

Open your notes and start answering the questions below in that order. Spend no less than ten minutes on each set of questions to really go as deep as possible and extract as much information as you can. That's crucial. It will be great to get a friend who knows you very well to ask for additional information later. Sometimes, other people have a better perspective than ourselves due to the lack of emotional attachment to certain circumstances in our own lives.

Okay, let's start now.

Spend as much time as you need to answer each question. Dig deep and write as much as you can. We are looking for both quality and quantity here.

STAGE #1: WHAT ARE YOU VERY GOOD AT?

What were you very good at when you were a kid? What did you often get praised for? What are you very good at now?

STAGE #2: WHAT DO YOU LOVE DOING?

What have you always loved doing? What makes you the happiest when doing it? What did you do during the most exciting moments of your life?

STAGE #3: WHAT DOES THE WORLD NEED?

What does the world need the most? What do people in your country, city, neighborhood, community, family need the most?

STAGE #4: WHAT CAN YOU BE PAID FOR?

What profession, product, service can you get paid for?

STAGE #5: WHAT ARE YOU WILLING TO STRUGGLE FOR?

What are you willing to give up? How much are you willing to struggle for what you want to achieve?

STAGE #6: WOULD YOU DO ALL THAT EVEN IF YOU HAD ALL THE MONEY YOU WOULD EVER NEED?

What if you became successful and generated more money than

you would ever need? What if you didn't have to work another day in your life? Will you still want to do that every day?

Notice how meaningful the system is.

What you get paid for mixed with what you are good at is most people's profession. That's the most boring place in the world, where 99 percent of people spend their lives. If you are there, I invite you to consider switching very soon. Life is too short to spend 80 percent of it doing something you don't love.

What you are good at mixed with what you love is what the Western world calls passion. That's what most people quit their jobs for and end up failing miserably. Why? Because the world doesn't care so much about you. People care more about themselves.

What you love and what the world needs — that's what some call purpose or mission. That's what most volunteers are doing, and it's amazing. I have great respect for that. The problem here is this: Let's say you volunteer but have no savings and are nowhere near financial freedom. One day, a family member gets sick and needs expensive surgery. But you have no money, and your loved one is left without life-saving medical care … I don't want to be in that position. Do you? Because life happens, and you want to be prepared for anything. I don't say there's anything wrong with volunteering, don't get me wrong. Quite the opposite. I just say that I also want to be responsible for the security of my family, which means I could never devote all my time and resources to this part of the system.

What the world needs mixed with what you can get paid for — that's the so-called "calling." That's the fake purpose. My first big business was precisely that for me. You are doing something great, you are making money, but it's not your thing. It took me five years to wake up and realize that I wasn't where I wanted to be.

Then there is the first addition to the original ikigai. It is: "What are you willing to struggle for?" What's the deal with struggle? Let me tell you exactly where this came from.

Maybe you remember the first part of the book, where I was about to decide to quit racing. I used to believe that I made this decision because I didn't want to put my family in financial danger and because of the dirty politics in the sport. That turned out to be only partly true.

Years later, I realized that there was a much deeper, more powerful, subconscious reason for which I decided to quit racing. And it didn't have anything to do with the external world. It was all about me.

You see, I was in love with this sport. I was learning and growing faster than most other racing drivers around the world. I was good. If I'd continued, I might have found a way to start making decent money. I was so in love with this vision of me being a Formula 1 racing driver. But ... I was not in love with what it would take to get there. I didn't love being on the road for 80 percent of the year. I didn't love spending much of my days at the gym. I didn't love the idea of running around asking for sponsorships — in fact, I never did. I loved to race. But that's not how the game was played. There was a different spectrum of struggle involved. A struggle that I was not willing to accept. So I looked for a way out. A good enough reason to quit. And I found it.

It's crucial that you analyze the pain and the struggle of the game you are about to enter. Everybody wants to be a winner, but not everybody is willing to play every type of game. I want to have the body of a fitness model, but I'm not willing to spend that much of my time, energy, and focus on fitness and nutrition. It's not the game I've decided to play. On the other hand, I've always felt that part of my Mission was to save and/or improve as many lives as possible. So whenever life presented me with this opportunity, I could stay awake for days and go through all kinds of crap to succeed.

You must pick your pain and be happy with it. Sounds controversial, I know. But there's no Mission without pain. There's no life without pain. You must know what you are willing to experience before you decide what Mission you want to build your life around for the next years or decades.

Mark Manson wrote, "No matter where you go, there's a five-hundred-pound load of shit waiting for you. And that's perfectly fine. The point isn't to get away from the shit. The point is to find the shit you enjoy dealing with."

Whether it's twelve hours in the gym every week, late nights in the office, or being away from home half of the year, you need to know what struggle awaits you and whether you are willing to accept it, experience it, and even learn to love it to continue growing in your Mission.

The last stage is something I'm a firm believer in. What if you succeeded? What if your Mission made you rich beyond your boldest expectations? What if your life and the life of your children was settled forever? Will you still go for it? Will you follow through on your Mission?

You see, most people ask the opposite question: "Would you still do it if you never made a dollar out of it?" But I find that quite unrealistic, which obviously makes the question useless. You must be much more interested in learning whether you will continue your Mission journey if you became the richest person on the planet. Because if the answer is "No," then that, my friend, is not the Mission you are looking for. There are so many examples of people who lose motivation when they get their first fat paycheck. Don't trick yourself into following the wrong path.

Warren Buffett said, "Look for the job you would take if you didn't need a job. Don't sleepwalk through life. That's like saving up sex for your old age. It's not a good idea."

I can't argue with that.

So let me give you an example of what an SMS might look like so you can get a better idea of how to complete yours:

STAGE 1: WHAT ARE YOU VERY GOOD AT?
As a kid, I was great at singing, writing, keeping things systemized and clutter-free. I then became great at racing, leading people and teams, motivating and persuading.

STAGE 2: WHAT DO YOU LOVE DOING?
I love spending time with the people I love. I love saving and transforming people's lives. I love speaking, writing, teaching. I love experimenting with new tools and strategies. I love creating new, meaningful businesses. I love learning and growing.

STAGE 3: WHAT DOES THE WORLD NEED?
The world needs a sense of success, vibrancy, and excitement at the same time. The people I know need to be inspired. They need to take action despite their fears. They need to know what their Mission is, and they need to live that Mission every day. They need to build financial freedom. They need to know how they can create happiness for themselves and the people around them. They need a system that they can follow that makes all that possible.

STAGE 4: WHAT CAN YOU BE PAID FOR?
I can get paid for products and services that generate massive, measurable, and transformational results for people.

STAGE 5: WHAT ARE YOU WILLING TO STRUGGLE FOR?
I am willing to stay locked up in my home for a year to write this

book. I am willing to experience the stress related to this goal. I am willing to give up my old identity of a businessperson for this period of my life. I am willing to accept all weird questions like, "When are you going to start working?" with a smile and move on with delivering on my Mission.

STAGE 6: WOULD YOU DO ALL THAT EVEN IF YOU HAD ALL THE MONEY YOU WOULD EVER NEED?

Yes! In fact, I can afford to write this book without working for over a year because I sold my business.

So here's what my Mission has been for the past year: "I'm going to create the most valuable system (this book) that helps people design and live successful, healthy, and exciting lives."

That's it. Now, check this out:

1) I use all skills that I consider myself to be good at.

2) I spend most of every day doing what I love doing the most.

3) I create what I believe the world needs the most right now.

4) I deliver based on demand. I'm not going to create something that you don't value or need. This means that while I keep on doing this right, I'll be able to sustain the message.

5) I'm aware of what it's going to take, and I've accepted it all with open arms.

6) I know that even if I were a billionaire, I would still want to be sitting at home, writing these words to you.

Now, if your dream is to create a hairdressing shop, you have the skills and the passion, but still, there are four more around you … well, what does the world need? You tell me. Be creative. How can you make this shop the most amazing experience for the clients? How can you add much more value and fulfill additional needs other than just cutting people's hair? I'm sure you can come up with some extraordinary ideas that might well end up making your shop the best in the whole world. I'd personally love to be able to get a massage and hold a business mastermind group meeting while having my hair cut. I love combining stuff to save time. So if you ever create that, send me an email. I'll be your first client.

I'll give you one more example in case the hairdresser didn't do the magic for you.

Think about what Elon Musk did. Did the world need another space company? No, not really. Nobody seemed to even care about space anymore until Musk shared with us his vision of sending people to Mars in the next decade. Now, did the world need to go to Mars? Not yet, I guess. But here's the trick. That's not what Elon Musk and his SpaceX were selling to us. It wasn't the trip to Mars — it was the excitement that humans can and will be a multiplanetary species. Does the world need such excitement? Hell, yes, it does! Was the world ready to pay to keep that excitement alive? Not at first. Musk had to develop different services, like bringing satellites to space, to get the money to develop his bolder Mission. How do you think it would've been possible to lure in the best talents that have the skills to make that grand vision a reality, if not for the "what does the world need" part? No chance! But that's what brings you your competitive advantage. You must start creating what the world needs.

My friend, you don't need to create a space company. You don't even need to build a business. But you need to design and follow your Mission — whatever it is for you. It's the only way to join the 0.1% Club. And you need to start now. Let me show you why.

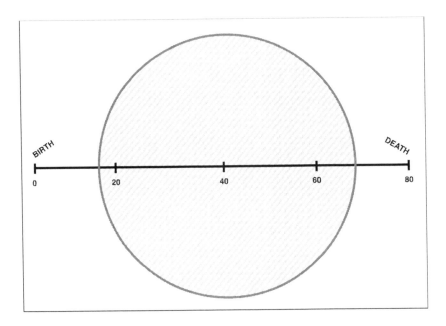

That's the life of a regular person. You are born, you start working at about twenty years of age all the way until you are almost seventy. The average person dies ten years later. Now, what do you want to do with these fifty working years of your life? It obviously takes a considerable piece of the whole. Do you want to spend it doing something you don't enjoy? Do you want to spend it hating on the Mondays and waiting for the Fridays?

Once these years are gone, they're gone. There's no turning back. **People ask, "What's the meaning of life?" or "What's my purpose?" You don't have a purpose! Life has no meaning! Not until you design it yourself.** Steve Jobs wasn't born with the idea of building Apple. Your Mission in life is to design your Mission and to live it every day. It doesn't matter what it is. It could be being the best janitor in the world or becoming the first Martian citizen. It's your Mission. You design it. You live it. But start living it now! Because the bus called life is waiting for no one.

TAKE ACTION NOW

(1) Complete your first draft of your SMS now. Then discuss it with people whose opinion matters to you (avoid the doubters and those who seem to have given up on their dreams). Get feedback. Then spend a week in your world, observing, thinking about how this Mission might play in your life.

(2) Once you are certain that it's the right choice, pull the trigger and go all-in on your Mission. Don't be afraid of the initial uncertainty. What you start with now might and most probably will change to fit with the constantly changing world and your constantly growing experience and knowledge. If you realize you've picked the wrong Mission somewhere along the way, you can always change it. It's your life. You can do whatever you want with it.

How do you feel, my friend? Any sparkles in the chest already? I'm so excited for you!

If you are pumped and ready to kick some ass, you are going to love what's coming.

Let's get a little crazy with...

9

THE GOALS

My wife and I were still only eight months dating when we thought of playing a little game. We would each separately sketch an image that would represent our biggest dreams.

We were sitting at the table in her parents' house in the little town of Pomorie, Bulgaria. It was a freezing October night, but you couldn't tell by the images we were sketching on the white sheets of paper.

I was having a lot of fun. I sketched an image of a beautiful house with a great Los Angeles view (it didn't look as great on paper as it did in my head). Teodora and I were in a swimming pool, and behind us were our kids, a boy and a girl.

An hour passed, and we were done with the drafts of our dream images. We compared them and were surprised to see that we both drew the same main things (a house with a beautiful view toward L.A., both of us married, and two little children — a boy and a girl).

We had a great time doing that. After we were done with dinner, we folded the A4 papers in our luggage and went to sleep.

Five months later, I moved to Los Angeles (where she already lived), and we started living together. A few things happened that same year. We got married in one of the most beautiful places on Earth, and we bought a house with a beautiful view toward L.A. Oh, and Teodora got pregnant.

Wait a minute! What's happening here? both of us thought.

We dug out the old sketches and put them on the table. We were both stunned!

Both Teodora and I knew we would sketch a house in L.A., because we had discussed that it was one of our dreams. But we didn't have an idea what the other was going to draw. When we looked carefully at the images, both of them had two kids — a girl and a boy. What was even more interesting was in both images, it was obvious that the kids had no age difference ... and ... my wife was pregnant with fraternal twins — a girl and a boy.

When we were drawing those images, I had no idea how I was going to afford to buy such a house in Los Angeles so soon in my life. I knew I wanted to spend my life with Teodora, but we were still only eight months dating. And never in this world had I thought I would be so lucky as to be the father of twins.

But that's what I sketched on that paper. And that's what Teodora sketched too.

Little did we know that things didn't stop when we folded those sheets of paper into our luggage. Secretly, both Teodora and I went on to implement those dreams in our visualization practices. And both of us included those sketches in it.

So for over a year, we would wake up, and one of the first things our eyes would see would be these images. Teodora and I together; our beautiful house in Los Angeles; and our amazing kids, which we never realized were twins.

And now all of that, our biggest dreams, were a reality.

My drawing

You see, you don't have to know how and why things can turn into reality to be able to dream about them. And you definitely don't need to minimize the size of your dreams to accommodate your current circumstances.

Having a deep desire and a crystal-clear, inspiring direction is the first step toward creating the future you want. Without that, you are leaving your life journey to randomness, and in most cases mediocrity.

So, my friend, it's time we put SMART Goal-setting to sleep.

Don't get me wrong. SMART (Specific, Measurable, Achievable, Relevant, Time-bound) Goals can be great and useful, but only for short-term, everyday goals.

If you use SMART for your mid- to long-term life and professional goals, you are in for a nasty surprise.

SMART Goal-setting will kill your dreams and your Mission!

That sounds cheesy, but it's true. Why? Let's consider the following: 99.9 percent of the world uses SMART Goals. That's good, right? It means it works ... Wrong! That means if you do the same for your mid- to long-term goals, you will be competing with 99.9 percent of the world. And that's just tough, my friend!

Do you plan on growing your new business 10 percent next year? That might sound great to you, and it's not bad, keeping in mind most companies die anyway. Right? Wrong! Think again! Do you want to create a thriving company or a company that just struggles to survive? I know what the second one feels like. My brother and I have been through years where we were barely able to pay out the salaries to our team. And that feeling sucks. People who perform at the highest levels don't operate like that. And that is why they compete in an area where there is only 0.1% of the crowd. A lot more room to breathe there.

What you really want is your business/salary/contribution to grow 50 percent or even 100 percent next year, don't you? So why are you afraid to put this as a goal? But we'll get back to that a little later.

SMART Goal-setting is stupid and boring.

When you were a little kid, you were a master of something really important that you later forgot about: visualization. You woke up, and your day started with a crazy, unrealistic vision of you being Batman or Wonder Woman or whatever you liked to imagine you were for the day (I was Spider-Man). Were you tired? Were you bored of just another day in front of you? Did you say "Oh, crap! It's Monday again!" I doubt it. Why? Because you had a crazy vision, and you believed you were this superhero and you could live in greatness right now. All it took was a little belief.

Today, you are a lazy bastard (don't ask me how I know) who needs a kick in the ass just to be able to get out of bed in the morning. And then you need to drink five coffees to make it through the day. Why? Because you are being SMART ... because you read that article that preached how being unrealistic is bad for you. But I'll get back to that later as well.

Don't be SMART! Be SMURT!

When I realized the truth of this dangerous lie that schools and society have been engraving into our souls, I got a *little* upset. And I took action straight away. I started visualizing again. Every day. And just for the sake of experimenting and playing it full out, I put several super crazy, unrealistic, but very inspiring goals in my digital journal and started reading them out loud every day (morning and night).

So instead of SMART, I now started using SMURT Goal-setting. I switched the "Achievable" to "Unrealistic" and the "Reasonable/Relevant" to "Resourceful." This was not the usual "ask from the universe, and it will give" journey but rather "ask from the universe and get to work, and then it will give." For some funny reason, they forgot to include that second part in *The Secret*.

Specific
Measurable
~~Achievable~~ Unrealistic
~~Relevant~~ Resourceful
Time Bound

A few months into that journey, "the universe" started giving. And it was giving me everything I was focusing, strategizing, and intensely working on. Things that I was scared to ask for before. Things that everyone laughed at when I shared what I was doing — like this book you are reading or the house I told you about.

So instead of keeping on being SMART, here is what you can do:

Instead of fighting with 99.9 percent of the world, set a few Mission goals that are far beyond that bar. Set a goal that the top 0.1% have already achieved (it's still realistic for someone). Is it 50 percent growth next year? Or maybe a 100 percent salary raise? Make sure that it is completely unrealistic (for you), and you have no idea how to make it happen. Make sure you don't have the skills to make it happen. And make sure you have a very strong WHY behind it. Why do you want this so bad? Why is it important for the quality of your life and the lives of those around you?

Once you put it in writing, you'll get your brain to work and start figuring out a few fundamental things:

1) What do you need to learn to make it happen?
2) What do you need to do to make it happen?
3) Who do you need to become to make it happen?
4) Who do you need to meet to make it happen?

I guarantee you one thing. If you start setting and working on your SMURT Goals, in one year you will realize that setting this 100 percent growth goal now was actually pretty realistic.

There is no growth and excitement in this little box that everyone is trying to put you in, my friend. Don't look for what most other people do. Or even better — observe what 99.9 percent of others do, and do the opposite. You'll thank me later.

Instead of waking up like the lazy bastard you are (I'm just messing with you, I know you are super-energetic every day), get a little crazy. What have you always dreamed of? Forget about work and business for a second. Do you want to build the most advanced school campus for orphans? Do you want to travel the world, making money from your laptop? Do you want to buy a sailing boat and spend a few months of the year riding the waves? Find the best partner in life? Whatever it is, materialistic or not, if that's what you've been dreaming of and it will add significant value to your life, put it in your daily visualization as a SMURT Goal. And make it a crazy, unrealistic one.

How different is every day if you look to the future with such excitement? And if you know that no matter how unrealistic this goal looks, at least you are working toward achieving it. Doesn't it change who you are today? Doesn't it fire you up more? Doesn't it make you alive?

This is how all of us must live every day of our lives. There's no excuse for being dreamless. Start being smart and stop using SMART when it comes to your mid- and long-term goals.

Once you start your new exciting journey, there will be those 99.9 percent who will have a good laugh at you at first. That's great! Welcome to the Club, my friend! Know that you are not alone. The laughter your goals provoke means only one thing: you are doing it right.

Let's be realistic (for real) here for a second: 99.9 percent of us want to change the world (or at least live exciting lives). That's reality. But the other part of reality is that nobody did that by setting realistic goals and planning for a mediocre being. You won't either. And that's as far as reality goes for you and me.

Here are some of the objections you will hear and what my reaction to them is:

"Oh, how badly you will hurt yourself when you fall from so high."

Really? Well, how badly do you hurt yourself when you fly so low every day? I am aware that I might not achieve 100 percent of my "unrealistic" goals at the desired time. And maybe I won't ever achieve some of them (I have some really crazy ones in that journal). Maybe I won't find the right path or strategy to make it become a reality (even though I believe I will). But at least I live with passion and pride, knowing that I'm trying to create something meaningful. And even if I achieved 50 percent of my SMURT Goal, it will still be several times more than what most other people will do by achieving 100 percent of their mediocre SMART Goal. I find more value and fun in my approach. Don't you? The great Michelangelo said, "The greater danger for most of us is not that our aim is too high and we miss it, but that it is too low and we reach it." No one enjoys playing the easy game. Excitement comes from the bold journey, not so much from the final achievement.

"Be realistic! People will think you are crazy."

Well, that's exactly what I'm looking for. I don't want to be like "people." I want to create my own journey, which is exciting, full of challenges and most importantly, hope. That's the energy that will pull me forward. Others have done it. I can do it too.

"Great achievements are not for everyone. You know that most people fail."

Yes, I know that most people fail. But I also know that it is not those who failed that felt sorry for themselves at the end of their lives. It is those who never tried.

"Stop being so greedy and selfish. You cannot have everything!"

How is wanting to grow as a human being, make my dreams a

reality, and expand my life experience greedy and selfish? Oprah once said that you cannot give anything you don't have. The more I make of myself and my life, the more I'll get to share with others and help them do the same.

Here's a very important lesson:

When people are trying to bring you down, it's because of their own fears and doubts. Because they don't believe *they* can make it. Their doubts have absolutely nothing to do with you. So keep on going. Some will follow your example and join your exciting journey, and you will help them do it too. Others will prefer to stay where they are forever. And all that is really none of your business. You are already on your way to the life you want to create.

Let's be hard dreamers and hard workers! We have nothing to lose and everything to gain.

I'll show you how to put this practice to use in the next STEP of the book.

Now, let's put all of what we've learned here in…

10

THE INTEGRATION

"If I manage to hit my goals next year, I'll move to Asia," Tim said.

"Why do you want to move to Asia?" I asked him.

"Well, it's the only place in the world where I feel at peace. I love the way people treat each other. I love that they are not greedy and envious of other people's possessions. I find myself much more inspired, calm, fulfilled when I'm in this environment. It feels like home," he shared.

One year later, I called him. "Hey, Tim! What's up? How were last year's results? Did you hit your goals?"

"Hey, Simeon! Everything's fine. The year was great. I did much better than projected," Tim started.

"So what happened to Asia?" I asked in a serious tone.

"Well, I really need to push for a few more years. You see, we started this new brand, and I'm now expanding it to a few more countries in the region. Maybe I'll be able to move in the next five years," Tim said with a sense of discomfort.

I knew what he was going through. I was there myself. Tim

was thirty-five years old and had been running his own business for the past decade. He started it because he needed to make money, and this niche seemed like it had good market potential. And it did.

Through years of dedication and hard work, he managed to prove himself and transformed his life from barely having enough for living expenses to now sitting in the back seat of an expensive black limousine with a personal driver. He was a successful businessperson, by all measures. But he was miserable. And he was well rooted to continue being that way.

"Tim, why do you really think you want to move to Asia?" I asked him with a clear idea of my follow-up question.

"Because I really love the place. It makes me feel great. I'm happier there," he said.

"Don't you think you are happier there because it keeps you away from doing things here that contradict with your values and personality?" I continued.

"Well, I don't know," he mumbled.

"Can it be that you are focusing on achieving results that are not aligned with your values and with what could be your true Mission in life?" I asked, because I already knew the answer.

As you might have noticed, being my friend is not always a pleasurable experience. But hey, you got this book, and you've come that far, so it's too late for you. Keep reading, my friend!

I've known Tim since we were kids, so I really knew what I was doing here. He is a passionate, loving, creative man who goes out of his way to help another person in need. He is a real self-starter, a ball of energy and positivity if put into the right environment. He has this deep, complex character that is always looking for ways to learn and improve from everything his eyes see. But now he was stuck.

His business was nothing more than a cash generator. His goals were nothing more than numbers on a page. None of his days were filled with excitement and vibrancy. They were all filled with a relentless drive to sell more of the same — his soul (values) for cash. He didn't believe in his product, and he didn't give a damn about the market.

Worst of all, to be successful, he needed to do much that didn't align with who he really was. He had to create and sustain relationships with people he didn't respect and quite honestly disliked. He had to make controversial deals. He needed to constantly take actions that were damaging the dormant, true character within himself.

Tim made a fundamental mistake, which most of us do. After he achieved his initial goal of obtaining a certain amount of money (which was great), he forgot to step back and refocus. What was initially a healthy motivation was now nothing more than a guaranteed way to keep on living a miserable life.

It wasn't Europe that was his problem. And Asia was not the savior either. It was the circumstances that he created in his life through his business, through his goals. He made it inevitable to meet and be around the wrong people, to do the wrong things, to experience life in a way that brought misery instead of happiness.

All he needed to do was to step back and ask: Who do I want to be (The Values)? How do I want to experience life? He needed to start from there, not from the business goals. After answering the first questions, he needed to redesign his Mission (The Mission) so it aligns with those values. Only after these two steps did he need to create a set of new, inspiring goals (The Goals) that correspond with the true Mission and values.

You see, we are so focused on the end result that we forget that we are rowing in the wrong direction for most of our lives. We start with "I want to make a billion dollars" or "I want to become famous" or "I want to have a huge house with a swimming pool" and move on to build fake Missions and broken Values around these dumb Goals. And these fake Missions and broken Values lead to nothing else but miserable lives, even if we were to achieve all those Goals and many more.

We cannot run away from our inner self and our values. We can pretend as much as we want, but if deep inside we value honesty, every time we disrespect this value we will deplete our reserves of self-respect and happiness.

In the same way, we cannot run away from our true Mission. It's there inside of us. It's always waiting to be appreciated and acted upon. If we don't bring it out to the world, if we don't do our best, it will turn into an ever-expanding bubble of regret.

Start with your Values (Being) and build your Mission (Doing) and Goals (Having) from there.

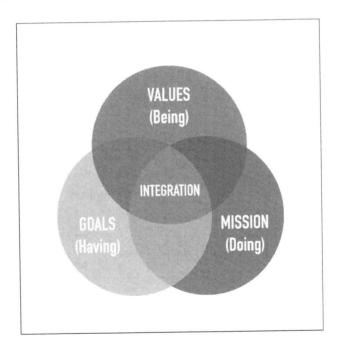

Look at this simple graphic. If you follow your true Mission but without practicing your true Values, there's obviously a misalignment. If you reach your Goals without your true Values — well, that's just more of the same crap. If your Goals don't align with your Mission — yep, same. If you have the Values but follow a stupid Mission — same. If you have the Mission but don't move your ass to achieve your Goals — same. Everything must be in alignment for an Integrated Being. Most people focus on having and achieving without realizing the importance of being and then doing the right thing.

Aligning the three areas is the only sure way for Integration. If you are in a position where you will need to change course (just like Tim), welcome to the club. I've gone through that several times in my life, and I'm sure I'll need to do it many more times before my time is up. Same goes for everybody else.

Don't get stuck in the past. The choices you made months or years ago were based on the past circumstances. If you didn't have money, it is only natural that you picked the first, fastest route to making some. Just be honest and allow yourself to change direction to the life you most desire to experience now.

Stop paying so much attention to what other people will think when you make the change. Nobody knows what's best for you but you alone. Nobody knows what you value. Nobody knows what Mission aligns with your heart. Damn, we don't even know those things before we dive into analyzing and extracting them from the deepest parts of our soul. So stop listening to bullshit opinions and start designing your personal, integrated strategy for Being, Doing, and Having. There is no other way to live a truly great life.

Tim didn't need to move to Asia or to become any richer to feel more inspired, calm, fulfilled, and to find people who treat each other with respect. He needed to be honest with who he wanted to be and then set his Mission and Goals in a way that will align his life with his true Values.

You don't need to have a million dollars or to be at the top of your Mission to be the person you want to be today. Being is within us. It's not material, and you can experience it before you even begin working on your Mission.

Once you start living as an Integrated Being, the doors to the 0.1% Club will be wide open for you, my friend.

Wow, you've done a great job coming so far! Isn't it amazing to have this sense of clarity and purpose in your life? To know that you are designing your own journey the way you want to experience it?

Let's move on with STEP III. We are nearly halfway through to complete your system.

STEP III: THE SKILLS

THE POWER OF ACTION

"I fear not the man who has practiced 10,000 kicks once, but I fear the man who has practiced one kick 10,000 times."

— BRUCE LEE

Our lives seem so complicated. Since the new era of globalization and technological development, much of humanity has been given limitless opportunities for life experiences. This abundance of choices has distorted our attention and has pulled our focus from what matters the most to what we might perceive as new, interesting, important.

But even though the world has transformed, the set of Skills that you must master to enter the 0.1% Club has not changed dramatically. This goes to show that the Skills needed for a successful, healthy, and exciting life are not a secret, not complicated, not too difficult.

Let's dive into the world of your Character and equip you with the weapons you need to master every field of your game.

But first…

11

WHAT IT TAKES TO GROW

"I don't care if you have to crash to do that! We have just fifteen more minutes left in this session! I need you to do something! Because you don't do anything! You just do your laps! If you're going to do that, you better go stay in Bulgaria! Try something different, and then we'll see what's the best! Okay?"

These are the words of a world champion in karting, coaching me on how to approach snow on the racing track. I have almost no experience in rainy conditions. Snow on the track is quite a bit out of my comfort zone. But he's right. This is the last practice session before the qualification. I must change something now!

I try to leave my fears in the paddock and go back on track. I'll do whatever it takes to reach the pace of the leaders! But damn, it's so slippery! My guts are turning upside down. Every time I touch the brakes, the rear axle goes into a barely controllable slide, and my focus subconsciously switches from the corner's apex to the nearest barrier.

I must stay focused! It's almost the end of the session. Let's push!

I finish my first lap and look at the electronic dashboard on the steering wheel — new lap record. Second lap — new record. I'm starting to build up my confidence fast. I can do that! I can compete in these conditions!

I see the track marshals showing the one-minute sign; the practice will be over after this lap. Last chance to improve.

I reach the fastest part of the track, and I decide to break even later this time. And then … in a blink of an eye, I find myself flying sideways through the muddy grass … it's too late to do anything now …

My kart SMASHES into the safety barriers, and the engine dies…

I quickly move my fingers, my toes, my neck. I'm okay. I step out and walk away from the danger zone.

I walk back to the pits, but instead of the expected nagging, I get a huge smile and a pat on the back from the world champion. "You did an amazing job!" he says.

He's right. I'm so much faster than before and so close to the leaders now.

We repair the kart, and I end up moving from "Captain Slow" to leading one of the toughest karting competitions in the world. What a weekend!

My performance in this race caught the attention of Formula Renault teams, and I received several offers to test during the winter season. A few months later, I was already part of the Formula Renault Championship. This quick interaction with my coach changed my whole life.

What did it take to grow so fast during this session? It was one simple thing: pushing over the limit. Not to the limit, but over the limit. I learned this fundamental lesson in racing. **You never know where the limit is until you go over it. You never know what you are capable of until you take a bold step out of your**

comfort zone. Until you push yourself. And yes, sometimes until you find yourself buried under the safety barriers.

On the racing track, you don't have a lifetime to realize that you're failing. You have a single session, a single race, a single weekend. So your lack of courage and persistence becomes crystal-clear pretty fast. I'll show you how to use this micro perspective in your everyday life in the next STEP. I know you don't want your journey to pass in mediocrity. Nobody wants that.

How does my racing experience translate to real life? Think of it as walking that extra mile. Doing that extra rep. Picking up the phone and having that awkward, difficult conversation. Over, and over, and over again. Even when it hurts. Even when you're scared. And then analyzing and learning how to do it better, faster, smarter the next time. Every time. Act, fail, learn, repeat. Act, fail, learn, repeat. Until you succeed. And then level up your game once again until you reach a level where the air is lighter and the skies are clearer. A level few are willing to even dream of. That's the 0.1% level where you don't see traffic jams. Why? Almost nobody is willing to go through the struggle to get there. Most people prefer to take the easy road and live lives far from their potential instead of taking responsibility and starting their exceptional lives today.

You don't need to wait for years to see the results from your new way of being. You need a single session. A single push. A single step out of your comfort zone. Thus, you don't have to wait even a single day to start living a much more meaningful life, filled with much more learning, much more excitement, success, and fulfillment. It starts now. It starts with a single action. A brave action. It starts with you.

12

THE FIELDS OF PLAY

The game of life is not a single race. It's not our money. It's not our achievements. It's not our relationships. It's not our health. It's none of those things alone. It's everything. I've learned that the hard way. Even though I was a leader in different parts of the game, I always felt like a loser overall. I was losing in my life.

So what are the different fields of the game? What should we master? Where does it most matter?

I've found that the system is quite simple. It only has so many areas you must work on. And those areas are: Health, Relationships, Emotions, Mission, Money, and Time. Let's look at each one so you can get a picture of what I mean.

HEALTH

"Health is a state of complete physical, mental and social well-being and not merely the absence of disease or infirmity." This is how the World Health Organization defines health. Most of us think we're healthy when we're not sick. We compare ourselves with the averages in our already obese and sick countries, which in the best-case scenario can only lead to average (often poor) results. Let's use the true definition of health as a goal that can lift our energy levels and our vibrancy higher than we have ever experienced before.

RELATIONSHIPS

The Relationships field represents the quality of connection we are able to create and sustain with the people who are important in our life: intimate partner, family, friends, colleagues. It's the feeling of being a part of the right tribe.

EMOTIONS

The Emotions field represents our level of overall emotional stability. It's the peace, the joy, the happiness, the excitement we are able to experience on a regular basis.

MISSION

This field is all about purpose, performance, and contribution. When you look at what you do, do you have a sense of Mission, or does it feel like just a job that you must do to put food on the table? Do you have a sense of contribution beyond yourself? How well do you perform in achieving your major goals?

MONEY

The money field is ultimately about reaching financial freedom and a sense of security throughout your whole life. How do you feel about the financial condition of your household in the present moment? Does it correspond with the lifestyle you wish to have? How do you feel about the future when it comes to money?

TIME

The Time field represents your perceived level of ability to manage and enjoy life out of work and Mission. Do you have enough time to experience the things you want to? Do you take time to celebrate your life, your successes, your growth?

We spend much of our lives focusing on one or two fields of play and neglecting the others. I've personally focused on Mission and Money between nineteen and twenty-six years old, giving over 95 percent of my attention to these fields. I achieved many of my goals during that period of my life, but I never enjoyed the journey, which made the whole game pointless. I was not fulfilled. I was not excited about my life. That led to a serious emotional and physical breakdown. I was performing so poorly in all other fields: Health, Relationships, Emotions, Time, that when I look back to this period of my life, it feels like I've wasted all those years.

Other people go to the other extreme. They are all about "having fun" and "enjoying life," so they put most of their attention on Relationships and Time. Somewhere along the way, they find themselves in a place where everyone around them has "grown up" and is running a completely different type of life. And that's when it hits them that it's "too late" to make a change, and they dive into a personal identity crisis.

You'll notice that these fields of play are so interdependent that you cannot improve one without it having a positive impact on the rest. And vice versa. When one is hurting, the rest are being damaged as well. Think of it as a bicycle wheel where each of the fields is a single spoke holding the wheel's integrity and shape as perfectly designed. The moment you break a spoke, the whole wheel breaks down. That holds true for our lives as well.

No matter our focus, if we don't take great care of all fields of play, our overall game is going to hurt. Our experience of life will be far from our given potential. This was my realization. And this became my goal: implementing and mastering the simplest Skills to improve all areas of my life at the same time. I wanted to feel excited about life again. I wanted to be healthy, truly successful, and fulfilled at the same time.

What do you think your life looks like at this very moment? If your life was this wheel, how strong and balanced do you think it would be? If you must score your Health field from 0 to 7 (where 0 means you are dead, and 7 means you can't possibly do any better than that), what would it be? What about the other areas — Relationship, Emotions, Mission, Money, Time?

What is your level of satisfaction with each of these fields? Score yourself and fill in the wheel like the following example. You can download a template of the wheel from www.simeonivanov.com/products/book-course (section "The Skills") or fill it in on the next page if you are reading this on paper.

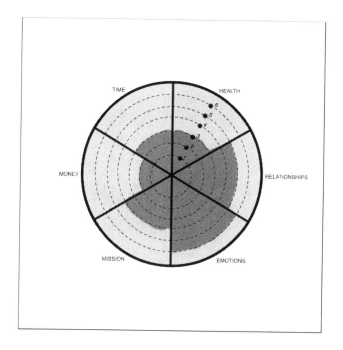

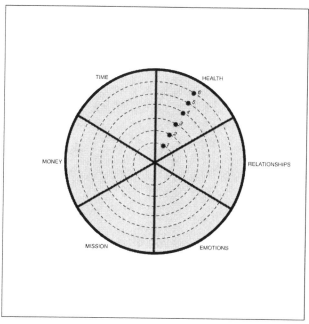

So, how does your wheel look? Does it look round and complete? Or are there a lot of imbalances and low scores? If this was a real wheel, will it help you reach the places you want in life, or will it break halfway through the journey?

Don't worry if it doesn't look great yet. Mine looked pretty crappy when I was starting off and still isn't perfect. But I'm getting there. And you will too.

Look at the wheel again. Do you feel that you've been giving your all until now? Where have you been making excuses? How will your life look and feel if you knew what you needed to do, and you showed up strong every day from now on?

This wheel is your life. Never neglect any of the areas in it. The bigger and more balanced the wheel, the faster you'll be able to reach the things you want in life. Sounds like a fairy tale, but it's true.

Right now, we're going to design your perfect game plan and equip you with the most important Skills that will transform each field of the game. These Skills are very simple. And you need to be great at the simple things to start living an incredible life. I'll prove it to you!

Let's do it!

13

THE BIG FIFTEEN

I used to do all kinds of useless and often damaging things to compensate for my poor performance in many of the fields of the game. Here are just a few examples:

I would sleep poorly and would be extremely tired and distracted. The solution that I invented? I would take medication that is usually prescribed for children with ADHD to boost my focus performance. The result of that was a short-term gain with extreme focus capabilities followed by a crash in performance the next day as well as some super weird experiences in my relationships with my friends and family. I would literally feel my brain burning like a steak and would be unable to hold a regular conversation with people. Overall, I would lose more time from the following day's loss of performance compared to the win that I got from the short-term focus gain. And I would damage my brain in the process. What a dumbass!

I would allow all kinds of distractions (phone notifications; calls; people coming in) to break into my daily schedule, crushing all my attempts to be productive. To "fix" that, I would just add extra hours to my work day when everybody else had long left the office and was already sleeping. This "brilliant" idea nearly killed me. I was lucky to meet a friend of mine (a doctor) who urged me to Google a Japanese word. I went home that day and remembered to check it out. The word was *karoshi*, and its literal translation is "death from overwork." I must have looked pretty bad in that meeting.

People do all kinds of stupid things trying to find a quick fix to their problems. I know some who believe they must go to ayahuasca retreats to heal their weaknesses, become superhuman, and get closer to their more spiritual being. At the same time, they take zero care of most of the fields of play and haven't even meditated for three days in a row. That example is not too far from most of the world drinking several cups of coffee every day to energize their bodies and minds while constantly eating junk, sleeping for only five or six hours, and spending zero time working out.

Here's something new: there is no quick fix. It takes years to mess up our minds and bodies, and it will take a little while to repair the damage and get to new levels of overall performance. And we won't be able to put these fires out by adding more fuel to them. However, if we implement our systems (which we will) and start practicing the whole set of Skills that I'm going to share with you here (which we must), our growth will compound extremely fast and will spread to every field of the game like wildfire.

You were born with everything you need to live an incredible life. You don't need expensive drugs or fancy gadgets to be great. Hell, you don't even need coffee to feel energized. What you need is to practice the Big Fifteen Skills every single week for the rest of your life.

Your greatness lies within this set of Skills. Your extraordinary abilities are there. Your happiness. Your health. Your success. Your entry pass to the 0.1% Club.

If you are not a master of the simplest of things, you must forget about all crazy "advanced" techniques. But if you do become a master at those simple Skills, you may never need to learn any others to be able to get everything you want in life.

Make no mistake — my goal is not just to share what will help you get to the 0.1%. That's what most books do, but they fail to help you actually implement those things in your life. In the next STEP of the book, I'll show you how to always do those things that matter so that you never stop growing. When we set up your system, you will never have to worry again that life is too complicated and you don't know what you need to do and when you need to do it to keep on growing instead of taking steps back.

If anything feels too overwhelming, don't worry. We'll take care of that in the next STEP of the book. Just stick with me.

Remember, simplicity is the friend of every person who's found his way to the 0.1%. Complexity is our enemy. We don't just want to know about the things that will level up our game. We want to live them every day.

Let's dive into the key Skills that will make your life a masterpiece!

SKILL #1: THE SWEET DREAMS

Most of us underestimate the importance of sleep. Here's a simple reason why you and I must take it much more seriously.

Have you left yourself to dive deep into sleep deprivation for a couple of days? I have, and it wasn't pretty.

During the initial growth stage of our first company (I call it initial stage, but I actually mean two to three years), my brother and I often worked until 4:00 a.m. That was the norm.

One week I had a massive project to complete and insufficient time left — just three days. I put on my suit (no idea why I wore a suit that day), went to the office, and started hustling. Three days later, and just fifteen minutes before the deadline, the project was submitted just in time. There was a little more to that story, though.

I didn't sleep for those three days. Not even a single minute. I was at the office the whole time, working on this project. I'll skip the details about how I smelled on the last day, but I'll share with you what I learned about sleep.

On my way to my car, I started shaking. I was beginning to lose consciousness. I stayed there, in the parking lot, all by myself, and I couldn't move at all. Next thing, I started hallucinating. But not the happy kind of hallucinations. I started seeing some pretty nasty stuff, and it was hardly midday. My brain was projecting my worst nightmares during daytime. It was sending me a perfectly clear and extremely loud message: "Give me some sleep now, or else…"

How important must it be for our brains and our bodies to get good sleep if the reaction is so powerfully adverse? First, you start feeling drunk, and then you start living your worst nightmares while still awake. The brain will do anything to get you to go to sleep. Why? Because you must!

I've since gone through some of the most recent research about sleep and decided to test every possible habit that might benefit my good night's rest. I've tried supplements, mobile apps, breathing techniques, superfoods, exercise routines, gadgets. Several years later, I've found a simple set of principles that, when combined, can provide great results. Today, these principles help me achieve significantly more during my day, and they boost my emotional and physical health to heights I've never experienced before.

PRINCIPLE #1: THE GOLDEN HOURS

We are all wired in a different way when it comes to sleep, but one thing is for certain: everybody has their golden hours and is affected by the biological influences of the circadian rhythm. Golden hours are those hours where it's best for you to go to sleep and wake up. It's critical that you find yours if you want to get the best out of your sleep. Here's what I did to find mine.

At the beginning of my test, I started going to bed at 11:00 p.m. and waking up at 7:00 a.m. It felt awful, even though I was sleeping much more than before. So I started playing around with these times, testing each fifteen-minute point on each side for a couple of days to see the difference. By moving with fifteen minutes on both ends, I found that my best range was between 11:00 p.m. and 6:00 a.m. It was much easier for me to sleep one hour less and to wake up at 6:00 a.m. than at 7:00 a.m. Weird, but a fact.

Similarly, you must start testing and find out which hours work best for you. You might be surprised.

Note that if you change time zones, your golden hours will change as well. My 11 to 6 didn't work when I moved from Bulgaria to the U.S. I had to start over to find out my Los Angeles golden hours.

PRINCIPLE #2: MAKE THEM STICK

Once you find these golden hours, make them stick. Do what you can not to go more than ten minutes earlier or later than your chosen hours. Keep this routine for a minimum of five days a week, every week. I use mine from Monday to Friday and let myself sleep an hour more and go to bed an hour later on weekends (if there's a meaningful reason to do so).

PRINCIPLE #3: NO SCREENS

Turn off all screen thirty minutes before sleep. No TV, no chatting, no Instagram, and emails. Have you seen a baby looking at a phone screen? You get my point. Screens are addictive and make your brain work like crazy. They suppress the release of melatonin (the natural sleep control hormone) that leads to increased alertness and arousal. We don't want that before going to bed.

PRINCIPLE #4: DARK AND COOL

Make the bedroom as dark as possible. Cover any blinking lights that you cannot remove from the room. Install darker and denser curtains.

Keep the temperature in the bedroom around 65F/20C. If your feet are cold, put some socks on.

PRINCIPLE #5: PHONES OUT

Keep your phone out of the bedroom — best to put it in Airplane Mode. There are three benefits to that. First, you avoid the exposure to electromagnetic fields. It's still debated whether it is harmful or not, but I prefer staying on the safe side. Second, you avoid the possibility of your drunken friends calling you at 3:00 a.m. You can set your alarm and increase the volume so you can hear it from the other room in the morning. Finally, you cannot hit the snooze button while half asleep.

My brain used to play tricks on me when my alarm would go off, and my internal voice would give me this "amazing" idea that if I slept on the other side of the bed for ten more minutes, I would feel much more rested … That's not a joke. Our brains will use all the tricks to keep us in our beds when tired. The same thing happens when you run, and your brain suggests it's a good time to give up because you might get hurt, while in reality, you are at 50 percent of your capability.

PRINCIPLE #6: NO SLEEP HACKING

Now, this is a critical one. There are people out there promoting sleep hacking and bragging about their three and four-hour sleep routines and how they can teach you to do the same thing. You'll do yourself a huge favor if you avoid following any of those suggestions. I and many others around me have learned that the hard way.

While there are people who can function well on such a crazy schedule (short hours or several twenty-minute naps instead of core sleep), 99 percent of us can't, not because we are lesser human beings but because nature decided our bodies will behave as they were naturally programmed to.

I've personally tested different sleep hacking techniques and have seen other people do the same. The result? It doesn't work for almost any of us. Not only does it not work for increasing your energy or productivity, but it harms them, and it compromises your health.

Moreover, if you are planning to test including several naps instead of core sleep, think about how that would fit with your everyday life.

"Honey, hurry up. We need to catch the plane."

"Uh, sorry, it's time for my second nap."

If you miss a nap, it feels like you didn't sleep all night. While you might be excited about geeking out at getting your naps right every day, think of the impact this might have on your social life.

If it works for you — great. If you haven't tried it yet, consider all the above before you do.

All in all, get more sleep. Most of humanity nowadays doesn't have enough sleep. If you are like most people, you need to get between seven and nine hours of sleep. Don't go below that unless you have tested it and you feel significantly better when you sleep only six hours. Very rarely will that be the case. If you happen to be one of those people, test sleeping for one or two hours more for a week to compare.

HOW TO - SKILL #1

So all you need to do is find your golden hours and set an alarm to remind yourself to prepare for bed (thirty minutes earlier works best for me) and one for your wake-up time. Decide on your first sleep to wake-up range test now and set up the alarms for tonight and tomorrow morning.

I've never had a sleeping routine before implementing my system. When I started coaching friends how to use it, I realized no one had any. From our experiences, all of us would point to this Skill as a crucial one for winning the games we were playing.

Going to bed and waking up at the same hours and sleeping at least seven hours a day seems to be a natural set-up of our bodies and our brains. After all, we didn't always have electricity and candles, and there wasn't much we could do in the darkness back in the day (I know what you are thinking).

Implementing a routine has helped everyone I've seen double their daily output and more than double their happiness levels.

If you think that sleeping seven or eight hours is for losers, consider the following list of people who take sleeping very seriously:

Bill Gates (Cofounder of Microsoft) – 7 hours every night
Ellen DeGeneres (Host of *The Ellen DeGeneres Show*) – 8 hours every night
Jeff Bezos (CEO of Amazon) – 8 hours every night
Arianna Huffington (Cofounder of *The Huffington Post*) – 8 hours every night
Tenzin Gyatso (The 14th Dalai Lama) – 8 hours every night

Sheryl Sandberg (COO of Facebook) – 7 hours every night

Many of them started this practice long before we learned about their successes and long before the world began talking about the importance of sleep.

Now it's time for you to go back to basics and get your sleeping routine in place. Your body and brain deserve it. Your loved ones deserve it. Your Mission deserves it.

SKILL #2: THE BRAVE VISUALIZATION

"That's not possible, man! Be more realistic!"

I've always been a little overexcited when it comes to life. But only when I compared myself with the average. And for most of my life, the average was what was surrounding me: average dreams, average effort, average results.

These two sentences I just quoted were the mental food that was served to me daily. Whenever I got a brave idea, I would get shut down by whoever I was "stupid" enough to share it with. It felt as if something was wrong with me. *If everybody else thinks differently, then maybe I am being too naive?* I thought.

So I buried this braver part of me deep down where no one could see it. Not even myself.

Years were passing, and life wasn't getting any more exciting. Why couldn't I have something if I really wanted it? Why couldn't something be done if I really gave it my all? So what if I'm too young or inexperienced? So what if most people fail?

I was not going to spend the rest of my life dreamless! And neither will you!

Do you remember when we spoke about goal-setting in the last STEP? Yep, about how we must stop being SMART and be SMURT instead. That's one of our main Skills for joining the 0.1%. And we are going to use it every single day from now on to lift ourselves beyond the average thinking of the surrounding environment.

This Skill has only one single principle, but it is a critical one:

PRINCIPLE #1: DON'T BE SMART

You remember this one. Instead of using Specific, Measurable, Achievable, Relevant, Time-bound, you will transform your visualization to Specific, Measurable, Unrealistic, Resourceful, Time-bound.

HOW TO - SKILL #2

1) Make your list of five to ten SMURT Goals as a note in your phone or wherever you will have them with you at all times (I use the Evernote app). Start with what you most desire in your life and move down the list by priority. Don't be afraid to include things you absolutely know cannot happen. Just put in what you really dream of that will add significant value to your life. It can be a relationship, contribution, a car, a house, money, or any business or life-related achievement. Anything you can act upon.

2) Make each goal as specific as possible. Include images where relevant. If it's a certain amount of income, include exactly how much. If it's a house, how many bedrooms, square feet, floors, etc. If it's a car, what make and model, what color, which engine size, and so on.

3) Read through your list every morning after you wake up and visualize how each of the goals has already turned into a reality in your life. Dive into the feeling of what it will be like to have it. Experience the gratefulness.

4) Then move on with your day, focusing on doing everything you can to turn those into reality. When you visualize every day for a few weeks, noticing the right opportunities and actions will become automatic. It's just like consciously trying to look for everything in a red color around you right now.

5) Change your list as many times as you want. These are your dreams, your goals. Nobody can judge them but you. If you change your mind on anything in the list — just change it.

6) When you achieve any of your goals, put it in a separate list and keep it as a reminder that a great deal is possible when you practice this Skill and do the work. It's incredible to be able to see your "Accomplished" dreams list growing with time.

The only way to start making huge things happen is to learn how to think and dream big. If you don't think it, if you don't believe it's possible, then someone else will have it. It's not for you yet.

But trust me when I tell you this: **Getting ten times larger results in life is never ten times harder**. Sometimes it can even be easier than achieving much smaller goals. Why? Because it's only the 0.1% that are aiming so high. No one else is taking the actions that will get them there. So we'll be playing a much less competitive game.

Achieving what most perceive as extraordinary does not require a higher IQ. It requires an open mindset, Brave Visualization, and some strategic, hard work.

I don't know about you, but I rarely think that I'm the smartest person in the room. However, I'm now always the one who dares to dream the biggest. And that helps me achieve results that many others are still afraid to even wish for.

I don't do any extraordinary things. I'm not any better than anybody else. I just focus on my inspiring goals and take one small but meaningful step at a time that can help get me there.

My friend, I invite you to join the club of the brave. Let's start making life worth experiencing!

SKILL #3: THE POWER MOVES

Did you know that your grandma and grandpa moved much more than you do? In fact, they moved so much more that their bodies burned about five times as many calories as you do, even without the fancy gym programs and routines we now have. How come? Let's picture a few major differences:

They walked / We drive
Their lifestyle was physical / We swipe and click on a screen

They didn't need to go to the gym or do anything extra to get their healthy amount of physical activity. Their work and even time spent at home were physically active. Ours isn't. And that's a huge problem.

Human beings were made for movement. We were born hunters and gatherers, running, climbing trees, working with our entire bodies. Our bodies have also been designed in a way that movement is responsible for much of the internal waste management through the lymphatic system.

Unfortunately, the more we develop as a civilization, the less we move. Today, we can get much of what we need with a swipe of a finger. And that's amazing. What's significantly better, though, is when we keep the rest of the body, other than our thumb, active and in great shape as well.

Our physical and emotional states are closely linked together through the chemistry of the body. You can simulate the posture of fear and anxiety for five minutes and start experiencing them soon enough, the same way you can power-pose and boost your testosterone levels and thus your confidence and energy. If you leave the body stagnant or with too little physical activity, your emotional state will deteriorate too.

During my racing career, I used to work out nine times per week (two hours per workout). Sundays were my only full recovery days. Needless to say, working out was not my favorite activity after I quit racing. So I stopped doing it for a few years.

After I got fat enough and all my past injuries started piercing my body with pain, I decided it was time to get back in shape. But I couldn't do my racing workout anymore. I didn't want to invest eighteen hours a week in that. So I did boxing, then switched to kickboxing, then tennis, then weight-lifting, then gymnastics.

Here are the most important principles that arose from all the mistakes and all the incredible coaching by some of the best experts in the world of professional athlete performance. These principles will be your base for your Power Moves Skill.

PRINCIPLE #1: THE RULE OF RULES

There are thousands of different workout routines on the Internet and a thousand more in the various gyms around the world. But which one is the best? I've found that the best and most effective workout is the one that you follow. It's not as much a workout routine as it is a way of life.

So many people try something for a week or a month, and then they quit, saying it didn't work. No program works in a week or two. If you are committed to achieving results, you need to be patient and deliberate. I'm constantly relearning this lesson because I'm often guilty of rushing to get a result I'm after.

One of my best friends is a great example of that. He gets super pumped every now and then, he starts working out six times a week for a few months, gets all ripped and excited, and then stops working out for six months and loses it all.

So for all of us who have ever quit exercising, the rule of rules is: ***Never skip a Monday and never rest for more than two days in a row.***

That gives you a minimum of two to three workouts per week. It's no big deal. But more importantly, it gives you consistency, and that's what you need the most.

That's too little for you? Great! It's too little for me too. I work out five times a week (on a perfect week). If two to three is too little, you wouldn't have a problem committing to that, right? You wouldn't have a problem always following the rule of rules, no matter what, would you? Even if you don't feel like it. Even if you feel a little sick.

You see, intensity and frequency are important. Very important. I love getting to a higher level and pushing myself to work out almost every day. But what we must value even more is that we never stop. That we never skip a Monday and never miss more than two days in a row. Even if you fall out of your regular workout routine (I hope you don't, but I have a feeling that you might) — never skip that next Monday.

PRINCIPLE #2: EVERY MOVE COUNTS

We have grown into perceiving simple, everyday movements as a waste of energy and time. So when our spouse or friend ask us to get up and get them the salt or help them vacuum the place, we put on our Grumpy Cat face and get all stressed out. We would much rather sit on the couch and watch that TV show. And that's a huge mistake.

You see, every move we make counts. Just as our grandparents burned many more calories and exercised their entire bodies from merely following everyday chores and working, we can do it too.

So next time, instead of thinking how uncool vacuuming, throwing out the garbage, going to the post office, and washing the dishes is, look at it as just another way to exercise and get healthier. If instead you would be sitting on the couch doing nothing of high significance, get up and do what you need to do and add some more to your daily dose of healthy movements.

I used to be the biggest fan of full automation and delegation for all kinds of tasks (especially house chores). I've only invented this Principle when my wife started asking me to throw the garbage or help her out with different tasks around home. I learned to love doing those things instead of hating them, because I realized I'm actually exercising while I do them. It's a win-win-win. Happy wife, clean home, healthy me.

All jokes aside, move your ass more. Much more.

HOW TO - SKILL #3

If you have no workout routine, you don't know where to start, and you don't have a smartphone, I'll give you the three coolest, most fun workouts you can do every week to crush your Power Moves game. They are designed to make sure you are able to follow them, even if you are in a hotel room with no gym anywhere around you. It's a no-excuses workout routine that helps you get more flexible and increases your strength and stamina. The equipment you need will cost you nothing unless you want to buy some really nice workout shorts.

If you have a smartphone, simply download one of the many amazing fitness apps. I've been testing many of those to be able to give you an informed recommendation, and my definite winner is the "Nike Training Club" app. It's free as I'm writing this, and it's super professional and easy to use. I'm not sponsored by Nike, by the way.

For all pros reading these lines, bear with me, my friends. I'll get to your level in the next STEP of the book to make sure you are also pushed to and beyond your limits.

Here are the simple workouts I promised you.

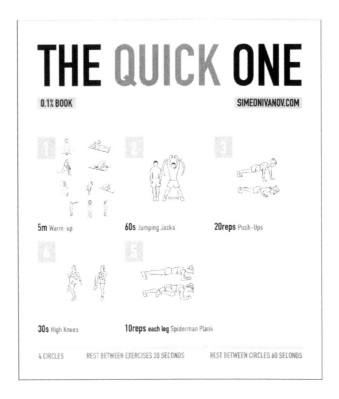

THE QUICK ONE

The Quick One is a four-round circle workout. You start with a warmup and stretching and then move on with the exercises. After you complete an exercise, you rest for thirty seconds before starting the next one. If you cannot complete the suggested repetitions, do as many as you can and build up the next time.

When you are done with step 5, go back to step 2 and work your way down again three more times for a total of four circles. This workout will take you no longer than fifteen minutes to complete. Do you have fifteen minutes a day? Yep. Let there be no more excuses for missing a Monday. You always have enough time for The Quick One.

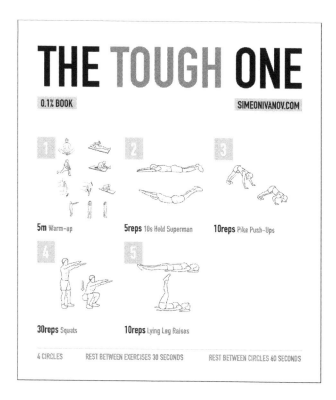

THE TOUGH ONE

The Tough One is your next level workout that is a great addition to The Quick One. Again, it's a four-cycle workout, it takes little time, and it's a bit more challenging.

Once you've completed step 5, go back to step 2 and work your way down again three more times for a total of four circles.

THE WET ONE

I know you'll love The Wet One. It's designed to make you out of breath and test your stamina at peak performance.

When you are done with step 6, go back to step 2 and work your way down again three more times for a total of four circles.

None of these workouts requires a significant time commitment. And they are absolutely free (I like great and free). When you practice them at home early in the morning, you won't spend more than thirty minutes to keep yourself in great shape. No more excuses.

If you have a serious reason why you must not do such training, I have you covered as well. Just set a thirty-minute timer on your phone and start walking, breathing, and stretching your upper body.

You can do that, right? Simply putting one foot in front of the other. One step at a time. That can be your lifetime workout that will keep you much healthier than most of the world.

The period from me implementing my system (about three years ago) till today became the first time in my life that I haven't stopped working out (except the racing years). Before that, I'd always found some excuse not to do it on a given day. And then the next day. And then the next month, which ultimately became the whole year.

For years I was struggling with my chronic inconsistency, which made me fat, slow, lazy, ill, and honestly, not too good-looking. But I realized it didn't have to be that difficult. I only needed to start by never skipping a Monday and never resting for more than two days in a row. This simple rule put me in the game for the long haul, and in no time, I found myself back in great shape, craving more physical activity instead of despising it. My morning workout became one of the best things for which I wanted to wake up early and start the day. From three workouts a week, I slowly moved up to four, and then a pretty consistent five times.

Did my new rule get me a six-pack? No. Not at first. But that was not the point. The point was to start and never quit. The point was to get in the game and stay in the game. To grow consistently and improve each field. There is one sure way never to get in great shape, and that is if you always quit. This rule is no workout program. It's a way of life. It's discipline. It's setting yourself up for success.

And guess what those little everyday successes lead to? Yep. More success. It's every small win, every little right action. It's the simple stuff. Can you promise yourself to work out two to three times a week? Of course you can. So do it! Do it now! Promise yourself you'll always follow this simple rule! I know you can do it, my friend.

Let's kick ass this Monday together! And if it's Tuesday today — well, what a great day to start as well!

Let's keep it fun and never step out of the field of play again!

SKILL #4: THE PRESENT MOMENT

My friend, how often do you get lured into a tornado of thoughts where you are doing something but your mind runs away from you and follows a different agenda? Do you sometimes find yourself emotionally stressed, overreacting, wanting to just run away? Do you often feel cut off from the surrounding world? I know how it feels. I was a master at that for most of my adult life.

My shower time in the morning would pass thinking about all the "crap" that awaited me. By the time I was ready to go to the office, my heart was already racing and my body was hurting in stress. That was my morning routine — kill the day before it has started.

It wasn't until I had a complete breakdown that I learned what was happening and how I could change this catastrophic way of living. I learned that the only way to turn around these stressful thoughts and emotions was to practice awareness and presence. How? Through meditation.

Some people tell me, "Yeah, but I'm not a fan of meditation." I know. Of course you're not. Eating pizza is so much more fun. I'm also not of fan of tooth-brushing, but I do it twice a day because life sucks if I don't.

Others think that meditation is this crazy spiritual act that is reserved only for monks or weirdos. **My friend, you don't need to become a monk or sell your Ferrari to get the benefits of meditation. It's not about living a spiritual life. It's about living a great life. It's about rising above that which is unimportant and living in a space of control. Meditation is not about becoming a person who wants and owns nothing. It's about becoming a person who doesn't get owned by anything.**

It's time to start meditating. I know you have a thousand excuses in your back pocket not to, but I really don't care about those. And you shouldn't either. I've heard them all. It's too difficult. It's not for me. I can't concentrate. That's exactly why you need to start doing it today.

There have already been over a thousand scientific studies that link a stunningly wide range of physical and mental benefits to meditation. Some of those are the reduction of stress, anxiety, depression, and the risk of health conditions like stroke, heart disease, even Alzheimer's disease. Researchers found that meditation significantly improves your mood, focus, information processing capabilities, mental strength, and can even reduce physical pain. Through MRI scans, some scientists have also been able to show how meditation increases gray matter in the brain. Do you ever feel that you need some more of that? I do!

Don't wait to be the last person to get on the boat. Almost all successful people are meditating already, and they don't do it for no reason. The future generation will most probably be obliged to practice meditation at school. I'm sure it will become as mainstream as working out, and it will happen very soon.

PRINCIPLE #1: YOUR MIND WILL NEVER STOP

"How do I make my mind stop?" That's one of the most popular questions when it comes to meditation. The answer is — you don't. Trust me. It's like wanting your heart to stop.

Many people believe that stopping the mind is the solution to their stressful emotions. They believe so because their minds produce garbage for most of their days. They believe meditation is supposed to make their minds stop. And when they see that they cannot stop their minds through meditation, they stop practicing it. Meditation is not meant to make your mind stop. It's meant to bring awareness to the work of the mind. It's meant to create a distance between yourself and the problems of everyday life, to help you see the bigger picture and to rewire and put your biological system back in perfect shape.

There's a great video in one of the guided meditation apps, Headspace, where the founder of the app, Andy Puddicombe, illustrates what meditation does:

> "An easy way to think of it is to imagine yourself sitting on the side of a busy road — the passing cars representing the thoughts and the feelings. All you have to do is to sit there and watch the cars. Sounds easy, right? But what usually happens is that we feel a bit unsettled by the movement of the traffic. So we run out into the road and try to stop the cars, or maybe even chase after a few, forgetting that the idea was just to sit there. And of course, all of this running around only adds to the feeling of restlessness in the mind. So training the mind is about changing our relationship to the passing thoughts and feelings. Learning how to view them with a little more perspective. And when we do this, we naturally find a place of calm."

All in all, it's about learning and relearning to see the bigger picture. To start living life with the deeply embedded knowledge that the sun always keeps on shining even above the darkest clouds.

So don't seek to stop your mind. Seek to become aware of its work. Once you start practicing meditation, you'll be able to point out your hidden fears, stressors, and anxieties, and they will become nothing more than just another thought passing through your mind. They won't control you anymore. You will be in control.

PRINCIPLE #2: CUT OFF THE MENTAL JUNK

When it comes to what the mind produces, it's what you feed it. So be wary of the food you serve to your mind every day. Cut as much as you can all news, negative talk, useless TV shows, sad and angry music. Substitute those with things that bring you up and generate positive emotions.

Meditation will work wonders for you, but if you are present and positive for 1 percent of your day and abuse the rest 99 percent, you won't really achieve any significant, lasting benefits.

I was mentoring a young man last year that was going through a serious nervous breakdown. Throughout our conversation he mentioned how life was difficult and emotionally painful.

I stopped him right there and said, "Tell me three interesting things you did last month."

He went on to explain how he didn't really do much because he was feeling so depressed. Finally, he remembered that he did go to a music concert with friends and also went to the park several times.

"Was life difficult and emotionally painful when you did those things?" I asked him.

"No ..." He mumbled.

"So where is life difficult and emotionally painful, my friend?" I continued.

There was a long pause.

"... in my head," he finally managed to conclude.

If you let yourself dive into ugly, automated thoughts, your life can become a living hell. But at 99.9% of the cases, there's nothing painful or sad about the present moment. In fact, there's a bunch to be grateful and excited for. You just need to become aware of that truth.

Meditation is the only known practice that will keep you away from the dangers of the unaware being. Sometimes, it can literally save your life.

HOW TO - SKILL #4

If you don't know how to meditate, I recommend you start out by using a mobile app like Headspace. I'm not associated with them or paid to say that. That's just how I started, and I still use the app occasionally to mix it up with my own meditation practice. Apps like Headspace, Omvana, and many more teach you the main techniques, so you can't go wrong by following their advice. Many of them have free meditations, so you don't need to spend any money to start.

The most popular meditation practices for people who already have some experience are Transcendental Meditation and Vipassana Meditation. You can Google these and learn how to practice them yourself. Even better, you can take a class at a meditation center; search for one with great customer reviews.

If you are advanced and want to go to the next level, do a ten-day Vipassana meditation retreat. No talking, no reading, no tech, no eye contact, definitely no sex, nothing. I did a three-day

experience that was organized by my wife, and it was mind-
blowing. You learn things about yourself and life that you don't get
the chance to learn in other activities. It's amazing how different
the experience is to everyday life. After all, we never really give
ourselves much time to be present and do nothing.

I find it extremely helpful to include a short gratefulness
practice into my meditation. Every time I sit to meditate, I start
with three things I'm grateful for. This reminds me that no matter
what I'm going through in my life, there is much to appreciate here
and now. Gratefulness is huge for anyone. Use it!

We'll include meditation in your complete system, but for now
you can start practicing it every morning for ten minutes. My
personal preference is to do it before I start working and once more
after I'm done working for the day. That helps me to switch to a
different mode and put myself in the zone I need to be in for the
hours ahead.

———

Realize that meditation is not only you sitting in a Buddha-style
position with your eyes closed. We could meditate throughout the
whole day if we wanted to. We could be in meditation state while
washing the dishes, while reading a book, while walking, working
out, even listening to others. Meditation is nothing more than
complete presence in the moment. And this presence is addictive. It
gives you a pleasant rush. It makes you more confident, more calm,
more grounded. It's a flow state that you get to experience
every day.

**Meditation is the only way to get in the 0.1%. Without it,
there is no way to stay in control and exploit the power of the
present moment. Without it, we all spend much of our journeys**

wandering off in the past or the future, where life is nothing but a distant memory or wishful thinking. These are two realms in which we have zero control.

Start meditating today and learn to live your days in the NOW. That's where the game is being played, my friend.

SKILL #5: THE SACRED BREAKFAST

The food we eat is the quality of fuel we provide to our bodies. It can be a healer, a boost of power and energy, or it can be our poison. And that's entirely under our control.

When I was six years old, I was diagnosed with asthma. The doctors said it was because of our German Shepherd, Sara. So my parents had to send away our beloved dog friend to my grandparents. But my symptoms didn't stop. A year later the doctors said it was the pollens from the trees. Autumn and winter came, but my symptoms were still there. Then they concluded it was because of domestic dust — and there was no way to prove them wrong here. Or was there?

I went through a four-year treatment where I had to be in the hospital twice a week to get injection shots in my triceps. Not the most awesome experience of my life, but it had some benefits. Every time I got the shots, it made my hands look like bodybuilder's hands. I thought that was fun back then.

Twenty years after the diagnosis, I read a ton of materials about food, supplements, and food allergies. I still had my asthma killing a few weeks out of every year of my life, but I had given up on doing anything more about it. Even the four-year treatment had not worked. But there was something new that caught my attention. Something I knew nothing about; doctors never mentioned it, nor did anybody else around me. That simple thing was a food intolerance test.

I signed up straight away and got the full package to get tested for every possible food there was. A week later, my results arrived.

I had a strong intolerance level to all types of dairy products, eggs, and gluten. Not a big deal, right? Well, not if that consists of a big percentage of your diet, which was the case for me back then. So I reshaped my diet that same day, and I started my new routine: no dairy, eggs, and gluten. I was shocked by what happened next.

My asthma was gone, and my nostrils cleared up from other allergies that I didn't even know I had. I could breathe properly for the first time since I was a little kid. My skin became clean, with no pimples for the first time since I entered puberty. All that took just a few weeks.

I decided to experiment further. I stopped eating red meat and sugar for two months. My stomach stopped getting bloated for the first time in my life. I lost much of the extra fat I'd gained in the past few years. I didn't feel sleepy after eating lunch. Instead, I was full of power.

I asked several friends to join me and take dairy, gluten, red meat, and sugar out of their diets. Their results were extraordinary as well. More energy, less fat, better skin, no bloated stomachs, elimination of lifetime allergies.

This experience opened my eyes to how much food was affecting our health. I went on to test different eating habits: vegetarian, vegan, pescetarian, ketogenic. I tried fasting, cleansing, detoxing. And I learned a lot. Mostly I learned how to listen to my body and the signs it gives me.

Many people tell me, "I feel good the way I eat." And I've been guilty of such comments as well. The truth is we have no idea how bad we feel or how much better we can feel and look before we try something new. We're just too used to feeling bad. That has become our default state of being.

From all the years of learning about and testing different eating habits, I can give a few critical suggestions that stand true for anyone. These are my own principles that I recommend to virtually anyone, implemented into this simple key Skill: The Sacred Breakfast.

Why breakfast and why sacred?

Breakfast is the first meal of the day. It's your first opportunity to win the nutrition game. If you are not killing it with your breakfast, there's no point in talking about diet at all. A healthy breakfast does much more than nourishing your body. Other than giving you the energy and power you need, it keeps your mind away from constant cravings, and it makes you feel like a champion for taking the best possible action first thing in the morning. This raises your confidence levels and sets the tone for healthier, smarter choices throughout the day.

Note that *breakfast* doesn't need to be a 6 a.m. meal. It's simply your first meal for the day. I know some people do intermittent fasting (which I love) or other programs that don't necessarily include an early breakfast.

If you are already crushing it with the rest of the meals in your day — that's amazing! If you are pumped about nutrition, and you are a master of this field — way to go! But if you're not, realize that The Sacred Breakfast is your entry level into the field of Health.

We are all aware of the extreme obesity, heart disease, cancer, and diabetes epidemic that societies around the world are experiencing. Yet many food manufacturers, restaurants, cities, and communities are still being designed to support this trend. What we end up with is a constant loud noise that pushes us toward the wrong foods and eating habits.

Processed junk that is packed with empty, unhealthy calories has become the cheapest and most widely available option and is on the rise. The bigger issue is that it has also been designed to become the tastier (to our senses) and most addictive option, since the leading manufacturers spend hundreds of millions of dollars to play with our biologically programmed cravings. The result? The annual sales of salty snacks and sweet sugary confectionary hit approximately $100 billion (with a B) in the U.S. We spend about 70% more on potato chips and cookies (or the like) compared to fresh vegetables.

Crappy food has become cheaper and more widely available than ever. This "lovely" trend has put the whole world at risk. Don't think that your country is not part of the picture. While in 2016 the U.S. ranked 12th (with a 36% obesity rate), other countries which are known for "healthier" eating habits rank as follows: Canada (29%); Australia (29%); United Kingdom (28%); my beloved Bulgaria (25%); Spain (24%); France (22%). Note that this is not the overweight rate but the obesity rate. Some projections point out that if the trend continues, half of the U.S. will suffer from diabetes by 2030. Ouch!

I don't know about you, but I prefer to live a life free of coronary heart disease, diabetes, cancer, and obesity-related conditions. I prefer doing what is within my circle of control to nourish my body for maximum performance and health. The greater our energy and health, the greater our experience of life. Without doing what's within our control to build great health, we can shove all our successes ... you know where.

So let's dive into the main principles and construct The Sacred Breakfast.

PRINCIPLE #1: LISTEN TO YOUR BODY

Nobody knows what you must eat but you. You must learn to listen to the signs of your body.

As a first step, I recommend that you have yourself tested for food intolerances. Many of us spend our whole lives trying to find the reason for much of our illnesses and allergies. We spend our hard-earned money on medication, supplements, and beauty products, yet the secret to getting rid of our problems often lies in limiting or getting rid of certain types of food. You must learn what's poisoning your body, my friend.

I personally did a test for IgG food allergies. This approach has not yet been 100 percent proven, but it did work wonders for me and everybody else I know who'd done the same test. When you go to get yourself tested, check the different packages. I made the mistake of paying for the most detailed one and later saw I didn't need to. Usually, the middle packages include 99.9 percent of the foods you eat. You don't need to know whether you have an intolerance to the seeds of the horned melon — unless you eat that every week. You get the point. Don't waste your money if that's the case with the packages in the clinic you visit.

Follow the suggestions that come with the results and listen to your body. You didn't spend money just to know what you are intolerant to. You'll feel and see the benefits in only a few weeks. If you end up having no food intolerances (which is rare), congrats and don't worry. I have other great suggestions for you.

By the way, if you think that those intolerance tests simply say stop dairy and gluten because they assume these are bad for most people, that's incorrect. I've seen people who are intolerant to tomatoes, and they felt amazing after getting them out of their diets.

If you think that the test is expensive, try to compare the two sides. On one, you have the one-time investment of the test, on the other you have your energy levels, sick leaves, all medication costs, and the quality of your life down the road.

If you don't have the money, there is one way that will take longer but will give you 100 percent correct results. And that's testing removing foods from your diet one at a time for fourteen days. Remove eggs for fourteen days and change nothing else in your diet. Keep a journal and write down the effects of the test. Then reintroduce eggs for seven days and remove dairy for fourteen days. And so on.

If you want to do the food intolerance test (be smart and do it), go to your calendar now and schedule an hour to research and book an appointment. Don't leave it for "someday," because you will never do it. Someone once told me, "Someday is not on the calendar." I checked. He was right.

PRINCIPLE #2: EXPERIMENT WITH EVERYTHING

Test taking other potentially harmful foods out of your diet for at least two weeks. Sugar is the obvious one, but other foods like red meat and eggs might also prove to be bad for you.

Listen to your body again. It will tell you whether that's a good or bad move. If you feel significantly better without it, leave it off the menu. If after two weeks you feel worse or feel no difference, bring it back. Make sure you only change one thing at a time, and journal the experience to understand which food creates what difference.

PRINCIPLE #3: NO DAIRY

Take dairy out of your diet completely or limit it to just a few servings a week, no matter the results of your food intolerance test.

There are heated disputes about whether we are carnivores or herbivores. The truth so far is nobody knows. But there is one thing we know for certain and over which there must be no dispute: we are not milk drinkers. Cow milk is for baby cows the same way cat milk is for baby cats and human milk is for baby humans. Baby humans. Not adult humans.

There must have been someone extremely weird who decided to go under a cow and suck its titty. We are the only creatures in the world to have invented such an absurd possibility. And now it's backed up by large corporations that won't shut up on all media channels about the benefits of milk. There are some. Significant ones. But only if you're a baby human, and you're drinking human milk.

My friend, you don't need to believe any of that. I know it might be hard, because Bulgarian feta cheese is the best and it used to be my favorite thing in the world. But don't take my word for it. Just take dairy out of your diet for a month and see for yourself. Everyone I've seen doing that is experiencing significant improvement in the quality of their lives.

So stop being a baby cow and start living as an adult human. It's much cooler.

You can get more than enough high-quality calcium and protein from other sources. Also, there are a bunch of healthy substitutes for cheese and milk that taste almost the same. Ask Google.

PRINCIPLE #4: BACK TO BASICS

When we put animals in the zoo, what do we usually feed them? If there is a monkey, do we feed it cereal with milk? Or cheeseburgers with Coke? No, not really. We do our best to feed the animals whatever they ate in their natural environment. In this case, naturally grown bananas.

Why? Because if we were to feed them anything else, their life expectancy would shorten significantly and the quality of their lives would be ruined.

Modern medicine has made it possible to significantly drop mortality rates and has also increased our life expectancy. However, we are doing our best to pull this trend backward and not only shorten our longevity potential but also add massive damage to the quality of those extra years we are given.

How much of the food you eat every day looks like the food human beings were made to eat naturally? And how much of it is processed?

If you want to use up the maximum of your health potential, you must go back to the natural way of eating as much as possible: less processed and more organic, whole foods.

PRINCIPLE #5: SMART GROCERY SHOPPING

Health is bought in the grocery store. Fill the shopping cart (physical or digital) with more natural products and less processed foods. It's very simple. If you buy junk, you'll eat junk. If you don't, you'll eat healthy.

That's the place where we either win or lose the game. To make sure you win, only shop with a list of approved (by you) items and after you have eaten a very nice meal and you are full. Trust me, you don't want to leave your willpower to fight against your cravings for junk.

PRINCIPLE #6: MONOPLATE

The Monoplate Principle was introduced to me in 2007 as one of the main rules of my preparation for the racing season. Dr. Riccardo Ceccarelli, who is a Medical Doctor Specialist in Sports and founder of Formula Medicine, set a standard as part of my nutrition plan to put all my meals in one single plate. The reasoning behind that was simple: I could see what and how much I eat, making sure that I include everything important (carbs, proteins, fats, fibers) in the right quantity.

Dr. Ceccarelli's team and their training program got me in the best shape and performance level I've ever been in. My body fat mass at that time was 10.74 percent, which is considered very lean for pro athletes (normal for men is within the range of 18-22 percent.) They were not excited about that number and pushed me to go below 10 percent, which I did later in the year.

Even though this program was rather extreme, bearing in mind my goal to perform at such a level, many of its rules were based on research on healthy living and great performance that stand true regardless of whether you are a pro athlete or not. The Monoplate Principle is one such example that will help you reach new heights in your health game without needing to go crazy about calorie counting and deep nutrition knowledge.

As long as you keep a healthy mix of vegetables, fruits, fish (without heavy metals), nuts, and oils in this plate and avoid sugar, dairy, and processed foods, you'll be doing a decent job with your Sacred Breakfast.

PRINCIPLE #7: DO SUPPLEMENT

Supplement with multivitamins and/or healthy powdered greens every day. Also, check which vitamins you might be missing when taking certain types of food out of your diet, and add those as a supplement too.

I personally use Adam multivitamins by NOW Foods, and my wife uses Eve from the same manufacturer. From time to time, I take a break from the multivitamins and switch to Athletic Greens powder, which also provides digestive enzymes, probiotics, and helps create a more alkaline environment in the body. Both options offer a very diverse range of vitamins and are of great quality (not paid to say that).

HOW TO - SKILL #5

I'll give you a few superfood breakfast recipes as an example of what your Sacred Breakfast might look like.

Obviously, just like a training regimen, there is no one-size-fits-all diet. The best diet is the one that fits your individual needs and preferences and the one that you follow consistently. It's up to you to test and come up with your perfect plan. But whether you prefer pescetarian, vegetarian, vegan, paleo, or any other regimen, do follow this Skill religiously. It's your entry level to a much healthier life.

Play around to find the foods that work best for you and definitely have at least three go-to breakfasts that will save you from wondering in the morning and potentially making wrong choices.

The following recipes have been inspired by my days as a professional racing driver, being coached by some of the best specialists in the pro athlete performance field, as well as by researching the eating habits of people who live the longest and healthiest lives all around the world.

THE SACRED BREAKFAST – TYPE 1
Mashed Sweet Potato x 1/2
Can of Atlantic Sardine in Olive Oil
Cup of Kale/Spinach/Arugula
Extra Virgin Olive Oil 1 tbsp.
Multivitamin supplement
Organic Green Tea with 1/2 tbsp Coconut Oil

THE SACRED BREAKFAST – TYPE 2
Cup of Cooked Oatmeal with Almond Milk (unsweetened)
Handful of Almonds/Brazil Nuts/Walnuts
Banana x 1/2
Multivitamin supplement
Organic Green Tea with 1/2 tbsp Coconut Oil

THE SACRED BREAKFAST – TYPE 3
Avocado x 1
Extra Virgin Olive Oil 1 tbsp
Almonds x 20
Brazil Nuts x 3
Multivitamin supplement
Organic Green Tea with 1/2 tbsp Coconut Oil

When I first started practicing this Skill, I experienced several major benefits.

1) More energy throughout the day

2) Losing fat and gaining lean muscle mass

3) No bloated stomach, no pimples, fewer dark circles below my eyes

4) More motivation to make healthier decisions in every other area of my life

Don't underestimate the power of The Sacred Breakfast filled with the most important nutrients for your body. This Skill is fundamental, since it will pull all other fields of play to a higher level.

If you are already a master of this Skill, I'll give you the next level in the next STEP of the book. Until then, just make sure you crush it with your Sacred Breakfast.

SKILL #6: THE SUCCESS BLOCKS

Nothing significant and lasting can be achieved without a certain amount of focus and time investment. But focus and time sound way too conceptual for anyone to be able to do anything with them. Let's take this concept and make it actionable and valuable.

What is the best way to plan your day when it comes to your Mission? The answer: Success Blocks.

Your days are merely repetitive cycles in which you have the opportunity to achieve a certain amount of output. You are limited by time and your capability to plan, focus, and execute at a certain level.

So how do you become a top performer when it comes to that small part of your day — a single hour? You implement Success Blocks.

Success Blocks are one-hour chunks of your day in which you control the external environment to your maximum capability. Let me give you an example.

In a regular day, I might have one or two important meetings or calls I've scheduled in my calendar. Other than that, everything else in my schedule is Success Blocks. For example, I might have one meeting, then four blocks of book-writing and three blocks of marketing. Every block has been planned on Saturday (Skill #13: The Game Plan), and unless there is an emergency, it stays where it is without any changes.

What's unique about a Success Block? Compared to a regular hour of work, a Success Block is the most focused and productive amount of time you can possibly deliver in your day. Here's how you achieve that.

There is really no need for principles here, so we can jump right into:

HOW TO – SKILL #6

1) You eliminate any possible distraction. Your phone is on silent and vibration is off. You set a fifty to ninety-minute countdown timer alarm (depending on what works best for you), and you move the phone out of sight. You ask colleagues, friends, your spouse, not to disturb you before the alarm goes off and you stand up from your seat (unless the roof of the building is falling).

In professional sports, it takes fifteen to twenty minutes of focused mental and physical preparation to get into flow state. Once you enter that zone, you become a superhero compared to the usual you. That holds true for everyday work activities too. Different research points out that when you enter flow, you become two to five times more productive. I believe that the truth is somewhere in the middle. All you need to do is to shut down all distractions and really focus on the task at hand. Flow will come naturally as you build up your confidence level in the task you are performing.

How much more could you do and be if you were able to get into that state every single hour of your day?

But most people work in a distracting environment. And each time you get distracted from your task, you lose your flow (if you were able to get there at all), and it takes fifteen more minutes to get back to being productive. This also adds stress and drains your mental capacity.

Respect your Mission and your time and demand this respect from anyone who may happen to be around you. If you don't have a door and you work in an open space office, put on some noise-canceling headphones or comfortable earplugs and talk with all your colleagues. Let them know what you are trying to achieve and why. They'll understand.

2) You sit comfortably, and you close your eyes for thirty seconds to set the intention for this Success Block. "What is it that I want to achieve now? Why is it so important? How will it bring me closer to my end goal?" You remind yourself that whatever you are doing now, even if it is the most undesirable action of all (e.g., paperwork), it's part of the bigger picture. It's an opportunity to show your full potential. It's an opportunity to learn and grow. It's also an opportunity to meditate.

3) You sit for your fifty- to ninety-minute interval, and you do one thing and one thing only. And that's what you've planned for this block. No email, no browsing, nothing. Just your initially planned work. Even if you get distracted in your head for a second, you bring your attention back and get back to what you are doing. And you don't stop until the time is up. You simply do your best.

At the end of each block (after the alarm sounds), finish your sentence, your line of code, your last move of whatever you are doing, and stand up. Your next step is called Recharge.

4) Recharge is something you must never forget. Everyone who skips it loses a considerable amount of their capability to perform at a top level throughout the whole day. Recharge is very simple. You use the next five minutes to crank up the energy levels in your body and mind. You stand up, do some intense breathing, jumping, fast walking, dancing, while you listen to inspiring music (I know you might like them, but no sad songs allowed). That's your time to drink lots of water and go to the toilet. If you can get some fresh air in these five minutes — even better.

You see, it's not just about the time you put but the energy levels you are able to sustain throughout the day (and your life). Winding down with Recharge between short periods of intense work is crucial if you want to play the long game and win. Without this piece I call Recharge, you are making sure to drive yourself into burnout and cut a good amount of your achievement potential, as well as your life expectancy and life satisfaction.

5) After you are done with a Success Block and a Recharge, settle down and transition into your next Success Block with the right intention and energy. Never carry negative emotions or stress from one task to another. Transition smoothly and start with a fresh mind and an energized body. Then simply repeat all steps throughout the whole cycle of the day until you are done with all planned blocks.

Important notes:
When you are done with your Success Blocks for the day, you

are done. You'll notice that working like that will boost your performance by well over 100 percent. I manage to complete about three times more when I use this approach. Most other people experience the same results. What's important here is that you play the long game, seeing life as a marathon, not a sprint. Of course, there will be times where you'll be pulling all-nighters. But make those the exception and not the norm. You must keep yourself in perfect physical and mental shape to win.

If you've invested half your day working on your Success Blocks and nothing meaningful has come out of it, call it a day (have some fun if you can afford to do so). Sometimes you will have days when not much will be achieved. Instead of beating yourself up, think of what else you can do to make this day amazing. Maybe you can spend some more time with your family. Maybe you can go for a walk or work on your hobby. Whatever will make the day great — do that. And never feel sorry for not being super productive for a single day or two. That will happen. Take some active rest, rebound, and you'll be back in shape in no time.

I realize that you might not be able to implement Success Blocks because of the nature of your work. If you are in customer support, or you are a driver, a secretary, a doctor, or your job is all about meeting people and being outside, you might not be able to implement this Skill. If that is your case, you can still use some of the main principles to make your work day more effective.

You can put your phone on silent while at meetings. You can set the intention for every new hour of the day before you dive into the next task. You can do your best to plan the week ahead and keep your schedule organized. And you can and must Recharge as many times as you can, no matter the conditions of your work. If you have to do it in an open space in front of a hundred other people — who cares!? Teach your colleagues how to do the same and start a new healthy habit for the whole office. Everybody needs to Recharge. Never forget to do it!

SKILL #7: THE LIMITLESS ACTION

What are we ultimately aiming for? Results, right? And what creates results? Action does. But how do we never stop taking the right actions?

That's a billion-dollar question. How do we make sure we are always in action? How do we never stop playing the game? Even when it's tough. Even when we're scared. Even when we are on the verge of desperation.

What makes us take action? Is it motivation? Is it money? Is it love? Is it contribution? Is it fear of failure? Is it our personality? What is the key?

Let's observe.

Motivation is great. It's a major catalyst for action. It gives us the initial boost we need to start. But it's not always there. We are not always positively inspired. We don't always have a "gun pointed at our heads." So do we have to quit when we are having a crappy day? Do we have to wait for motivation to come back and save us? I don't think so.

There must be something else. Something even better than

motivation. Something that will help us start and keep going, no matter what is happening inside and around us.

Is it fear? Let's see.

Have you always taken action when you were fearful? I haven't. And I don't think you have either. Remember a time where you knew you needed to speak up, but you were afraid to do so? Did you raise your hand or find the "perfect reason" to keep quiet? I've been there a thousand times. Fear can be helpful at times, but it's not the ultimate answer we are searching for.

Money, love, contribution aren't either. All those things matter, but they are not the key.

So what is? What is this thing that will help us always take the right actions? It's the simplest thing of all. And the best part of it is it's 100 percent under our control.

The thing that can always keep us in action, the thing that will always pull us forward, the thing that will help us achieve the results we need is ... our word.

We spoke about honesty and responsibility earlier on. When we learn to stop bullshitting ourselves and others, we automatically grow into a new habit. A habit that has the potential of making us unstoppable. And that habit is called honoring your word.

When you start honoring your word, it won't matter whether you are having a great motivation day. You won't do things because you feel like it — you'll do them because you said so. You won't go to the gym because you feel energized. You'll pull your ass out of bed and put your training shoes on because you said so. You won't wait to speak up when you muster the courage to do so. Courage might never come without the action itself. You'll do it because you said you'll do it.

Those who achieve the most are those who act the most. And those who act are not always the most motivated ones. You don't have to be poor or experience any lack to take action. You don't need to be motivated to change the world to take action. There are millions of examples where people who had nothing to lose and everything to gain didn't do anything at all. Even when all boats were burned, and there was no turning back. The action-takers are those who know what they want. Those who make a commitment and then honor their word. They say what they're going to do out loud, and they simply go out in the world and do it.

Talk is not cheap, my friend. Not honoring your word is.

You don't need to change anything else to become a person of action. You simply need to say what you are going to do and do it. There's incredible power in that. Why? Because you only need to say something, and it's already on its way to becoming a reality. Because it's under your control. And when you teach your body and brain that this is how the world functions, you'll build the courage, the motivation, the self-confidence, the skills, the connections, and the knowledge to make your dreams a reality.

Start breathing power into your words, instead of your excuses, my friend.

We all know that procrastination is the main killer of all progress. And we procrastinate much more than we realize. You'll get a feeling of that when we are done with this book and you start running your brand-new system.

But what is procrastination? **Procrastination is merely the lack of action the same way darkness is the absence of light.** You switch on the light and BOOM! Darkness is gone. You move your ass off the couch and BOOM! Procrastination is gone. It's that simple.

I see people talking about writer's block, low productivity months, etc. And these things are real. They are as real as our decision to stick our asses to the couch.

There is only one cure for procrastination and low productivity, and that's action. Deliberate, repetitive, focused, simple action.

Just make the first step. Write the first word, make the first call, open the first project. You don't need to think of your project as this massive beast that you must encounter right now. No. You just need to take a single step. A single step is doable, right? You just need to put your sneakers on and head to the gym. Once you make this first step, everything becomes easier. And when you do it for ten consecutive days, you get rewired from where you are right now to someone who is a self-starter. A productivity beast. You just need to take your butt off the couch.

Make sure that whatever happens, you stay on the field where the game is played. Be a player and never find yourself in the audience, observing. The audience talks, the players work. The audience struggles, the players thrive. It's not scary to be on the field. It's only scary if you've been standing on the side for way too long. Push through this one time and never go back to that seat. Doing the right thing might hurt more today, but doing the wrong thing will bring pain for the rest of your life.

If the judgment of others is what's pulling you back, know that you are being judged anyway. You'll always be judged, no matter what. People judge. So take these excuses out of your system and start doing what you must do. That's your life. And you have only one chance to experience it. You might as well use the opportunity.

It doesn't matter what you did yesterday, last week, last month, last year. It's all about what you do now. The past is gone. The future will come. Focus on the present moment.

PRINCIPLE #1: PATIENCE WITH URGENCY

I had a dream a few months ago. There was a voice speaking to me, trying to convince me of something I didn't believe in.

"There is enough time," the voice said.

"No!" I shouted back. "No, there isn't!"

I woke up feeling like my heart was going to explode. I sat in bed and started thinking about that dream.

I believe it was my subconscious trying to pull me away from my Mission. I know there is time. But I'm never going to live with this belief without an important addition to it. I've built a mindset that works best for what I want to achieve. I call it Patience With Urgency.

Success takes time. It takes practice. It takes failure after failure after failure. It takes learning the lessons from each fall. It takes repetition. Thus, I learned to remind myself to be patient when it comes to major projects. That totally contradicts my personality, but I've learned to accept it.

However, you don't need to wait for everything in your life. After you have a great plan, you push the Start button, and you go for it. You can start learning today. You can start testing today. You can start improving today. You can start being the person you say you want to be today.

Yes, there is some time left for all of us. But we don't know how long. We are not born with a "use-by" date stamped on our asses. It might be a hundred years. It might be ten. It might be until tomorrow. Nobody knows. We must live today. We must create today. We must appreciate today. So, when our time comes, we can close our eyes for the last time and feel sorry for nothing. So when we take our last breath, we can say, "I lived with pride, honoring my principles and my Mission."

Do you think you lack the motivation to act on the things you want? Do you want to know how never to lack motivation again? Here's how.

You will die!

These three words are the most motivating thing in human nature. We will all die. And if you keep on saying that there is enough time to follow your Mission, if you keep on making five- to ten-year plans where you will work on your plan B before moving on to plan A ... you are in for a nasty surprise somewhere along the way.

Yes, we must build a safety net. We must sometimes do things we don't enjoy along the way to get to the place we want to. But we must work in the direction of our Mission, no matter what. Whatever weird job you need to get to sustain the Mission, learn the skills, put food on the table — do that! But do it for the Mission. Don't work on plan B. Plan B might fail just as easily as plan A.

What you see below is my life. I'm twenty-nine years old as I'm writing this. The black circles represent the years already passed. The empty circles are what's to come till I become a hundred. I plan to live to 120, but I want to make it look more realistic for those of you who think they only deserve to live to 80.

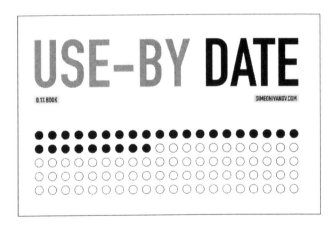

How old are you now? How long do you think you'll live? And until what age do you believe you'll be able to follow your Mission with maximum intensity? Without illnesses, without disabilities.

Open your notes and put down your own life in a little drawing just like that. You can also find an empty template of this image at www.simeonivanov.com/products/book-course   (section "The Skills"). Print it out and stick it to your door or your bathroom mirror. Or open it up every day from your digital journal to remind yourself how quickly time flies.

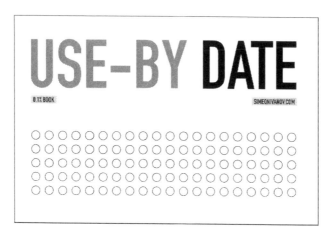

Next time, before you start making a plan B, check how much time of your life it might take. Is it worth it? Maybe it's time to put our years to work on what really matters.

When you have this little visualization hanging somewhere for you to see, it's much easier to give up the ordinary way of life you've most likely been living. It's much easier to stop making excuses for why things can't work, to start being more unreasonable (according to the majority), and start making things happen. When you develop such a mindset, doors will start opening for you. Doors that you haven't even seen before.

Next time you set a deadline for an important goal, divide it in half the time and start executing. You're going to do it in the last few days or weeks anyway, aren't you? Parkinson's law states: "Work expands so as to fill the time available for its completion."

When I first decided I was going to write this book, I figured it would take me about two years (I had absolutely no idea). I gave myself twelve months to complete it. The actual writing time it took me was six months, but I still took the whole twelve months to finish it.

My friend, life is in the challenges. In the struggles. No problems, no life. Don't try to reduce your problems. Don't hold on to the small ones, making your life all about trying to fix them. Don't look for excuses in those small problems for taking no responsibility. Try challenging yourself to counter larger problems, and the small ones will start taking care of themselves. Challenge yourself to chase problems that inspire you. Problems that deserve your time and your life.

Be patient, but waste no time! Practice Patience With Urgency!

PRINCIPLE #2: MAKE IT EASY-ER

Remove all clutter. Everything that is holding you back and adds no value to your life. Here are a few examples:

Terminate your cable TV subscription: Connect your TV screen to your laptop or phone and only watch what you want to watch, when you want to watch it. Make sure you feed your mind things that will help you with what you are trying to achieve. Don't leave it to random TV shows to decide what you consume. I haven't bought TV subscriptions for more than ten years.

Stop browsing with no purpose. If you have no good reason to go online, don't. Social media, news websites, blogs will do their best to suck you in and not let go until your eyeballs fall off. You might not know that, but some of those social platforms implement techniques that are used in casinos to benefit from the powerful science of addiction in gambling. Simply don't go online unless you know why and unless you set a time limit to your browsing sessions.

Make sure you consume information that will serve the specific major task you are trying to accomplish right now. Don't read books about how to create the perfect warehousing system if you must now learn how to generate sales. Read about warehousing when the time comes. Otherwise, you'll forget everything by then — trust me.

Next, clean your home and your office space. Sell or give away all useless products that you don't use (do that for real). Then buy some organizers for your drawers and your wardrobe and find a place for everything. Divide your stuff by themes, just like you would divide paperwork in your office — by color, by year, by date, by topic, etc.

The more clutter, the less performance. And don't tell me you have the soul of an artist. That's a silly excuse, and you know it. Just test being super-organized for a week and compare. I already know the results you'll experience.

The next important part of making it easy-er is to make it hard to do the wrong thing and easy to do the right thing. If you want to learn how to play the guitar, take out that guitar and put it on a stand next to the seat you use most. If you want to stop useless browsing, put a block on your laptop that prevents you from doing it. If you want to use certain apps only after finishing work, make a folder for all of them and put it five screens away from your home screen. By the time you've swiped to screen three, you'll already be getting a brain signal asking you not to act like an idiot. Do whatever you need to do to make it hard to be stupid and easy to be smart. For those of us who are a bit on the lazy side, we might as well use that characteristic to our advantage — we, lazy bastards, get very creative.

The last part, but not in importance, is this: learn when to say NO. Saying no to friends, family, even to great opportunities. Why do we need to be great at saying no? Because everybody has their own agenda. And everybody will try to lure you in their own schedule. If you allow this to happen often enough, your life is gone.

So what you can do instead, and what we'll do in the next STEP of the book, is set aside time for everything that is important. There will be time for friends, family, hobbies, but you will learn to stay on course and not get pulled out of your way. When it comes to opportunities, the more you take, the less focus you'll have. The less focus and time you put into your goals, the less the chance you'll succeed. So pick wisely. Learn to say no when saying yes will pull you away from your dreams.

HOW TO – SKILL #7

All we want to do here is to stop procrastinating. And that's not as hard as it sounds. As long as we are in action, procrastination won't be a part of the picture.

What I like to do is create triggers to counteract procrastination. Every time my ass touches the couch when I'm supposed to do something else, it's like I'm sitting on a burning stove. I jump right back up, and I pat myself on the back for doing the right thing. Then I'm back to work. The patting on the back might sound silly, but the truth is that it has wired my mind to switch on an alarm every time I start doing the wrong thing (which is quite often, by the way).

If I manage to go through my initially planned schedule without "finding my ass on the couch" at any time during the day, I know I've won. If I lie to myself and spend a few minutes (sometimes hours) watching Casey Neistat, Peter McKinnon, or swiping through Instagram during a time that doesn't say "Entertainment" or "Social Media," then that's a little failure that gets recorded in my system. No pats on the back here, and I remind myself to do better the next day.

That's what you'll be doing once you start your system.

Eliminating chronic procrastination from our days is one of the biggest wins in the game of life. It buys us our lives back. It buys us this forgotten feeling of self-worth. Our happiness. Our Mission. We all deserve to be great at this critical Skill. I'll show you how to become a beast at it in the next STEP.

SKILL #8: THE PURE WATER

How much water must you drink? It depends.

Where do you live? How much do you weight? Are you a man or a woman? How often do you work out? Do you have any medical condition? Are you pregnant? The list goes on and on. No online calculator can tell you exactly how much water you must drink, because that will depend on a hundred circumstances. But what I know is that there is a very high chance you should drink more than you currently do.

We all know about much of the important discoveries about water. We know that our bodies are made of about 60 percent water, and our brains, over 70 percent. Even our bones are made of over 30 percent water. It's said that the average human can survive almost a month without food but only a week without water.

We know that water is vital to keeping our bodies alive, energized, cleansed. I'd say that you must not drink less than 2.5 liters (85 ounces) of water if you are a woman and 3 liters (101 ounces) if you are a man. That's the very minimum in the average case.

The simplest way to determine whether you're drinking enough is the color of your urine. If it's close to colorless, then the quantity is most probably fine. The yellower it appears, the more dehydrated your body is.

Note that certain vitamins will make your urine yellower for a few hours after you take them, which is not a sign of dehydration. Once you start paying attention, you'll be able to distinguish the dye from the vitamins from the original color of your urine.

One thing I learned in my days at the gym is that if you are thirsty, you're already dehydrated. Don't wait until you are thirsty. Drink water every hour and keep yourself hydrated throughout the whole day.

So the overall message is: drink more water!

Of course, don't overdo it. Even the best thing in huge quantities can be toxic. There are reported cases of people who have died from overdrinking. But I'm guessing you won't be going crazy in water-drinking competitions. Unless that was the result of your SMS exercise...

Bear in mind that other drinks don't count for your daily water intake. And you want to eliminate those from your menu anyway. I'm talking about junk drinks like Coke, Pepsi, Red Bull, and the like. If you're thirsty, drink water.

If you want to take some caffeine, try mixing green and black tea with coconut oil and cocoa butter instead of coffee. You don't need the peaks and drops of coffee, which make you drink more and more to sustain the effect as the day goes on. Mixing the two teas with coconut oil and cocoa butter prolongs the effect of the caffeine as a smooth curve, rather than peaking and smashing you down in an hour or two (thanks, Tim Ferriss, for the great advice). Be careful, though, because this tea mix might also become too strong if you drink more than a couple of glasses.

When it comes to alcohol, it's time to get over it. I have no idea why cigarettes get such negative attention and alcohol doesn't (they both must). Alcoholism is a problem with a massive impact on the world, significantly surpassing heavy smoking, in my opinion. Alcohol can put you on the street in a month and kill you in a day. So if you stopped smoking (which you must), consider limiting alcohol to the absolute minimum. It was created with a medical purpose — use it as such. If you can't control your dose when you drink, stop it altogether.

There are enough broken families, poorly raised children, people on the streets, and many more who are no longer among us. Take some responsibility for your well-being and give a great example to everyone else around you.

HOW TO – SKILL #8

Put a few alarms in your phone to check out on your urine color tomorrow. Measure how much water you drink throughout the day. If your urine is not see-through, increase the daily amount of water until your urine loses its yellowish color (take into consideration the vitamins' dye). Once you reach the right amount, set it as your minimum for the day, measure it, and stick to it.

Note: Don't drink anything fifteen minutes before and after eating. You'll thank me later.

SKILL #9: THE INNER CIRCLE

Nobody is self-made. It's so funny when people brag about being self-made millionaires or self-made this and that.

It's high time we realize the impact that the people around us have on our lives. Who raised that "self-made" guy or girl? Who taught them at school? Who mentored them in their work environment? Who was there for them when life punched them in the face?

Nobody ever made it alone. And you won't either. Our inner circle (our family, spouse, kids, friends, mentors, people we work with) is our tribe. And we need a strong tribe to grow stronger. Just as in nature, the loners are those who will get eaten by wild beasts first.

But for some funny reason, many of us forget about our tribes because "we are too busy." And even in the days we do make some time for the most important people in our lives, we spend it poorly, without a plan for how to make it great.

Since we are going to start spending time with our tribe, we might as well learn how to do it better.

PRINCIPLE #1: SWITCH OFF

Why do so many people believe they must switch off their phones at work, but they shouldn't do the same while spending time with the people they love?

There are few worse things than constantly checking your Instagram or WhatsApp while you are supposedly spending time with another human being. Similarly, distracting yourself with anything while talking on the phone with someone you care for doesn't do much good.

Not only do you make the other person feel like crap (think about how you feel when someone does it to you), but you also scatter your attention, which stresses you out and ultimately creates a damaging experience for both parties.

If you are going to spend time with someone (face-to-face or on the phone), do it. If you can't be present, meet or call another time. And when you do, be there. Just like you will learn to fully focus on your Success Blocks, you will learn to do this with the people you love.

This is the only way to start building extraordinary relationships.

PRINCIPLE #2: LISTEN FIRST

You think that you've been listening to the people you've been talking to. I know that you haven't.

Every time the person on the other side says something, your inner voice starts asking: How / Why / Do I agree or not / Is this right or wrong / Is it good or bad / Is it true or not / Do I trust this person or not?

You are a machine made for judgment, trying to evaluate everything that's happening in the world based on your internal translation system.

Having an inner voice is natural. We all do. But if you are not able to distinguish it for what it is, you'll end up in trouble. Why? Because it prevents you from listening. Because it often tries to pull you down. And the only way to make it stop for a little is to show that you are aware of it.

You don't need your inner voice while someone is talking to you. You need to listen with your full, conscious being. You don't need to know the answer before the person finishes his/her sentence. And you definitely don't need to always feel in a hurry for the other person to finish so you can jump in and share your bits of wisdom. You love doing that, don't you?

Imagine that you've never really listened to anyone. Not your friends, not your spouse, not even your parents. If you haven't listened, how much of what they said have you actually missed? And if you've missed so much, do you really know them for who they are?

I know this answer. It's a NO. You don't. You don't know the people in your life for who they really are, because you've never listened to them without your inner voice interfering all the time. You've been "mind-reading," you've been "knowing" everything, and you haven't been learning what they wanted you to learn about them.

So guess what you'll do tomorrow? You'll listen. You'll know your inner voice is there, trying to jump in and interrupt, but you'll keep it quiet. You'll look into the person's eyes, you'll keep your mouth shut, you'll not walk around and do anything else. You'll just listen until the person has said everything they wanted to say, and then you'll leave three more seconds of silence, just in case. After that, you can have as much time as you want to figure out what you want to answer.

You'll feel that you are creating a connection on a much deeper level. Trust me, no one has listened to that person like you just did. Everyone feels amazing when you do that. You'll also be able to support them, because you'll finally understand them.

Listen! But really, listen!

PRINCIPLE #3: DEMAND A GREAT EXPERIENCE

When you enter a competition, what is your number one goal? To win, right? Or if not, at least to perform at your best. You demand performance from yourself because you cared enough to show up in the first place.

So why the hell don't you do the same in your relationships?

Start demanding a great experience with the people you connect with! And don't demand it from them — demand it from yourself.

How can I make this interaction enjoyable? How can I make it funny? How can I make it valuable for me and the other person? What is the energy I want to bring to this conversation?

These are the kinds of questions to ask yourself every time before going into a meeting, before picking up the phone, or returning home after a day at work.

Realize that you have tremendous control over the vibe in your tribe. Your energy, your spirit, your emotions will influence everyone else around you. If you make it your goal always to bring the best, truest part of you in this field of play, my friend, you will absolutely crush it.

PRINCIPLE #4: UNCONDITIONAL LOVE

What is unconditional love, and how do we get there? Many people talk about it, but very few actually experience it. Here's how you can reach that level.

First, you must stop looking for people to supplement your weak spots. My wife taught me that early on in our relationship. She explained how women and men usually look for partners who have something they don't. I hadn't realized how true this was before she explained further.

We expect so much from our partners, and often much of it is something that we're not. We expect them to be hard-working and successful, yet we are not. We expect them to be understanding and nonjudgmental, yet we are not. We expect them always to be supportive and caring, yet we are not.

When we look for partners with the expectation to fill a reality gap in our own lives, we set ourselves up for failure. What my wife taught people is to make a list of all those things they expected from a partner and ask themselves whether they were those things in the first place. And for all the qualities that weren't yet at the desired level, they would make an action plan and get to work.

If you demand a caring person, be caring first. If you demand a successful person, be successful first. Or at least give your all to get there. There's nothing worse than double standard relationships: "Love me while I don't love you." Never expect to find anything you are not.

Second, you need to take all equations away from the relationship. What do I mean by that? Usually, we play a little math game in our heads while experiencing our relationships with people.

If X happens, I'll take care of you. If Y happens, I'll show you love. If Z happens, I'll be supportive. That's called Conditional Love. If ... then.

Unconditional love is the love of a mother for her child (in most cases.) It's the love that has no equations. It is love based on principles, not on ifs.

Before you get into an intimate relationship, it makes sense to extract and compare value traits between both sides. You don't want to live with a person who doesn't share some of your critical values, the same way you most likely don't want to work or be friends with such people.

If you believe in monogamy and your spouse likes to play on the other side of the road, that can be a little problematic. But if you knew this before you entered the relationship, you could evaluate and make an informed decision whether you were fine with that or not. If you decided you are fine, and you went for it, then this topic is out of the equations. But if you didn't know and there was a breach of values during the relationship, then you must have a serious conversation with your partner about value alignment or a potential breakup.

Once you follow these two steps: (1) Become what you expect from others; (2) align critical values with the other person; then you will be able to engage in unconditional love. It's not something conceptual. It's absolutely practical and actionable. It's your ability to stay principle-centered at all times, no matter what the other person says or does. It's your ability to give love every day, no matter what.

Remember, nobody is perfect. People will get emotional, stressed-out, weak. But your actions are your sole responsibility. Make them count every day.

Remember that nobody owes you anything. Not even your kids do. Nobody is responsible for your well-being or happiness. Only you are. Every person is unique and leads their life both as an individual and as part of a tribe. Never try to take this away from people.

Finally, remember that the people you love are not going to be here forever. Too many people start sharing their true feelings months or weeks before they die. And so many others don't get the chance to do even that much. Don't be one of those people. There is no meaningful reason to wait. Tell the people you love that you love them. Tell the people you respect that you respect them. Tell the people you are thankful for how much you appreciate them. If this were your last chance, and you would never be able to see them or speak to them again, what would you like to share with the most important people in your life? Stop for a second, take your phone, and make some calls or write some messages — now!

HOW TO - SKILL #9

Practicing this Skill is as simple as spending at least fifteen minutes every day for the people in your inner circle (other than those at home with whom I hope you get to spend more). And not just spending the time, but really focusing on experiencing a meaningful interaction that adds value to your lives. Demand it from yourself before any call or meeting and then deliver.

Make a list of the five to ten people in your life that matter the most. Add their phone numbers on speed dial and make sure you get in touch with all of them at least once every week or two.

You see, being a part of the right tribe is as critical as oxygen. We were not designed to make it alone in this world. We are social beings. Without any human connection, we are as good as dead.

No matter how big your achievements, you need your tribe to

share them with. No matter how devastating your failures, you need your tribe to push faster through the pain. Find the people you want to share your life with. And when you do, give your best to make these relationships truly extraordinary.

SKILL #10: THE JOYFUL TEARS

My friend Pedja and I were having a meeting in my office where I was building this system for him from the ground up. We were at the stage where it was time to start developing his Skills. I asked him, "What was the one moment in your life that made you cry out of happiness and feelings of gratitude? That moment that made you feel that your life had great meaning, even if it was something simple. Where were you? What did you do? Why did you get so emotional?"

Pedja took some time to think and shared one of the best stories I've ever heard.

"I was with Nastya (his wife) in Serbia, visiting her grandfather in the local hospital. We entered the room, and there were three other men about the same age as him — somewhere around eighty. The guys were so funny, so amazing. We immediately started talking with all of them.

"I couldn't help but notice the conditions in the hospital. They were terrible. The beds and the sheets were old and dirty. There was some food left from their lunch, and I saw it looked and smelled terrible.

"I excused myself and went out. I remembered there was a pizza place just outside the hospital, which looked very good. I went to the restaurant, bought four large pepperoni pizzas, and brought them back to the hospital room.

"As I entered, I passed one pizza to each of the old men. I will never forget their faces. They were so happy, so grateful. They immediately opened the boxes and started eating like they'd never tasted anything like that before. I think maybe they really hadn't."

At this point in telling the story, Pedja was already crying and could hardly continue.

"So what made you feel so emotional? Why was that moment so special for you?" I asked him.

"Because I knew I made this day so much better for these guys. I made them happy. I had the power to make this happen, and it cost me almost nothing."

"Pedja, that's really amazing. Thank you for sharing that with me. When did this happen?"

"It happened a year ago."

"And when was the last time you did something similar?"

"I haven't done anything like that since that day."

Pedja was shocked by his own words. He was very well aware of the impact this simple act of kindness had on his life. He knew he had the power to repeat that time and time again if he only decided to. But then life happened and what brought him to tears of joy was now just a distant memory.

What if he was to start practicing that as a Skill? What if he was to plan and execute one random act of kindness every week? How much more powerful and fulfilling could his life become?

You see, we are so dumb that we forget to do the things that make us feel like our lives have meaning and value. We play busy and fill our days with useless moments instead of investing just a little time in creating meaningful ones. And I'm not here to judge. I'm as dumb as anybody else. I was there too. But why do we have to stay there? Well ... we don't!

PRINCIPLE #1: WHAT BRINGS THE TEARS

You obviously must analyze what those things are that make you feel so damn amazing that you can barely hold back your tears. Just look back and search through your memories. Then pick a few that really stand out and use them as your guide for this Skill.

PRINCIPLE #2: AS SELFLESS AS IT CAN GET

It's hard to name such an act completely selfless, since at the end of the day you do it because it makes you feel great. And there's nothing wrong with that. As long as you don't expect anything in return, that's amazing.

HOW TO - SKILL #10

Again, super simple. Instead of waiting for those moments to happen by accident once every couple of years, make them happen on purpose every single week. If you cannot come up with anything that amazing in a certain week (like buying a pizza for an old man), simply take the next random person who has done something good and have an honest conversation with them.

I once needed to go to the bathroom in an office building, and the receptionist pointed me to the right place. However, she also told me that if I ever needed to find one after work hours, I could go to the building next door, where they had one open (I must have looked very anxious). I simply took a minute to tell this woman how thankful I was for her taking the time to explain something that was not expected from her job. I told her how most other people would never step out of their way to help me so much and that I was sure this attitude would really help her progress in anything she wanted to do. She was extremely surprised and happy and went on to tell me about her kids and how she always wanted to help people out, no matter what job she did. I'm sure that short interaction created a lasting positive impact on her, and she also had a great story to tell her kids when she got home that day.

If you want to make something bigger, think of what your loved ones have always dreamed of doing and organize a little surprise for them.

I'd known for years that my granny's (seventy-six at that time) biggest dream was to drive a car. I could see how she looked at people driving cars, and she had this burning excitement inside of her, but also a feeling of regret because she'd never done it and now it was too late.

Well, was it too late?

All I did was take a day off, make a few phone calls, and rent a car with a passenger-side brake that cost me fifty bucks. I then got the car to an open lot and took my granny there. She had absolutely no idea what was going to happen.

Thirty minutes later and some seriously painful laughter in that car, my granny had one of her lost dreams turned into a reality. Honestly, I've never seen an old woman and her grandson so happy. Both of us had one of the best days of our lives.

My friend, it's time to start breathing more life into your days! Start with a simple, random act of kindness every week and write a life story worth sharing.

SKILL #11: THE PERSONAL UNIVERSITY

A student asked Bill Gates and Warren Buffett, "If you could have one superpower, what would it be and why?"

Here's what they answered.

Bill Gates said, "Being able to read super-fast."

Warren Buffett followed with, "I've probably wasted ten years reading slowly."

Why would two of the most successful people in the world care so much about what other people have written? Why would they spend a significant amount of their time reading — often consuming a book in a single day?

Try to imagine the following scenario for a second. How much more successful could you become if you started a company teaming up with Elon Musk, Richard Branson, and Arianna Huffington? How much happier could you become if your personal mindfulness coach was the Dalai Lama? How much more could you boost your performance if Tony Robbins was right by your shoulder every day, giving you advice? What if you wanted to become better at love and forgiveness, and you could call Byron Katie any time and ask for guidance?

And what about legends that are no longer among the living? If you knew that Mahatma Gandhi and Albert Einstein were hosting a dinner tomorrow night and all you needed to do was buy a twenty-dollar ticket to sit next to them and learn all the best lessons from their lives, would you sign up? Would you take the time to go and listen?

Well, you can. You can learn all the best lessons from the lives of the greatest minds who ever lived on this planet. And you can start now.

Some of the most precious treasures in the world are hidden between the pages of books. All the lessons are just a few clicks away.

All the great people that we so admire didn't become that great by chance. They studied and learned more than the rest. They read more. We must be crazy not to follow their lead here.

PRINCIPLE #1: WHY READ MORE, FASTER?

We all know how powerful books are. We know they stimulate our brains, help prevent diseases like Alzheimer's, reduce stress, and open doors to an unlimited knowledge source that leads to countless new opportunities. They boost our focus, memory, analytical skills, and obviously make us much better at communicating and socializing. Books make us smarter and cooler.

But if that doesn't motivate you enough, think about the following.

The average person reads approximately 200-250 words per minute and comprehends about 60 percent of what he/she has read. This same person's work consists of somewhere between three to six hours of reading every single day (that's the case with me as well).

So if, for example, I was to make $1,000,000 this year, about half of it ($500,000) would be money that I earned for reading.

If that's the case, what would happen if I learned how to read faster and comprehend more? The analysis of that question is quite clear. Advanced readers average speeds of about 400-500 words per minute (double the amount of average readers). What's more surprising is that they also have higher levels of comprehension of what they have read (over 80%).

If we were to invest a week in learning how to read faster and increase comprehension (there are a ton of resources on speed-reading online), and if we practiced this new Skill by reading more meaningful books ... well, we could start achieving similar results in half the time or double results in the same time.

We could learn twice as fast, we could achieve significantly more output, we could outperform much of the world.

If you were a racing driver, you wouldn't want to drive at 100km/h (62mph) all your life, right? Maybe you would if that was the first time you got in a racing car. But then you would want to go faster and faster, better and better.

Reading is the same thing. Don't read like you used to when you were ten years old. Learn how to read like a pro, and you will start achieving superior results.

PRINCIPLE #2: WHAT TO READ

Some people just read all over the place. And that's cool. It expands their vision, and I'm sure it helps with creativity. But if you really need to improve your sales skills now, you probably don't want to read *Fifty Shades of Grey* just yet (unless you are using some nasty selling practices I don't want to know about).

Read books that will broaden your knowledge in the fields that will bring you closer to your SMURT Goals. Read books that will help you develop the skills you need to increase your competitive advantage in your industry. Read books that will help shape you into the Character you want to develop. Read books with lessons you can apply now (not in a year).

And every now and then, treat yourself and read just to have some fun. If you've come that far, you deserve it.

PRINCIPLE #3: HOW TO READ

It's crucial that you don't read like most people do. Read like you are reading this book. Learn. Implement. Once you start your system, you will be able to implement any new Skill you want to add to your life. Any new habit you want to practice will become easily acquirable. But you need to make notes. You need to take the time and focus.

HOW TO – SKILL #11

1) Go to your calendar and schedule a Success Block to research and find the best speed-reading class you can take. Find one that works on comprehension as well. Sign up and schedule the first lesson in your calendar. Do it now before you move on.

2) Think of the top three things/skills you need to learn about and become great at to make your SMURT Goals easier to reach. Then go online and find the two best books for each of those. Get the books and decide which one you will start with. I'll be sharing and updating my own list of top books for each field in your free online course environment, which you can access any time at

www.simeonivanov.com/products/book-course in a section titled "What Next?" I'd be grateful if you shared the most valuable books you've read there too so the whole community could benefit.

3) Start reading at least thirty minutes every day. For those of you who cannot take thirty minutes to focus and read, get those books in their audio version (I use www.audible.com) and listen to them while in the car or while you are working out. When you park your car or when you are done with your training, make notes on the most important things you remember. You can always find thirty minutes one way or another. Don't make excuses! That's your life we are talking about!

I started reading quite late. I was nineteen years old. And I became a regular reader even later, when I started using my system, three years ago. Since that time, I have been able to significantly improve so many critical areas of my life. I became much better at being a manager, a leader, a salesperson, a writer (yes, yes, I was even worse), a lover, a parent, a son, a performer in the game of life. This system wouldn't have existed, and my life would've sucked big-time, if it wasn't for all the amazing books out there.

Reading is so much more than just entertainment. Use this gift to its maximum potential! It will keep the growth curve of your life pointing in the right direction.

SKILL #12: THE WEEKLY SURPRISE

She woke up, opened her eyes, and there I was, serving her favorite breakfast in bed. Some day the next week she woke up, entered the bathroom, and found one of a series of hand-written notes that were hidden all around the apartment. A week after that she received a beautiful flower bouquet at her office with a love note attached to it.

Does this sound familiar to you? Most relationships start this way. There is so much passion and energy in the first few months. You are willing to go out of your way to prove to the other person that you deserve them, and they must be with you and no one else ever again.

But that story I shared is not the beginning of a relationship. That's me and my wife, Teodora. And that's been going on since we got together over two years ago. I call it The Weekly Surprise.

Focus now, my friend, because this could be the one thing that saves your relationship or marriage from falling apart. If you follow it strictly, it could transform it from okay to a league of its own.

Most relationships start great, but 99 percent don't last, even if there was potential for a great partnership. Why? One of the main reasons is that once we "get" the person we want, we become super lazy. What was once exciting is now perceived as ordinary and boring. What we were once willing to do for this person to prove our love is now perceived as the so-called "pain in the ass" task.

BEFORE
"Honey, can you throw out the trash?"
"Of course, my love. I'll do it right away."

AFTER
"Honey, can you throw out the trash?"
"Hey, I'm not your janitor, okay!?"

Slowly but surely, we become increasingly stressed around that same person we love, and we forget why we got together in the first place. The time we spend together becomes quieter and less fun, and at some point, we find ourselves looking for a way out.

If you don't do any of the things that made this person feel loved, cared-for, special, how the hell do you think he/she is going to feel that way? And what do you think will happen with your own perception toward this person? If your actions show that you don't care (since no action shows that you do), what do you think will happen with the emotions between you?

Do you love someone? Do you want to make them feel great? Do you want to make sure that your relationships rocks and doesn't go down the drain? If the answer is yes, here's what you'll do from today on.

PRINCIPLE #1: LEARN WHAT THEY LOVE

If you've been so blind until now and have no idea what the person you are with loves, it's time to find out. What's the best way to find out? You guessed it! Ask. In an everyday conversation, simply include a question like "What are your favorite flowers?" or "What do you love me to do most for you?" or "What were the two things I've told you that made you feel the best?"

You see, The Weekly Surprise doesn't have to be a physical gift. It could be as simple as sending an out-of-the-ordinary text message or having an unexpected dance in a public place. It could be posting a great mutual photo with a lovely caption on Instagram. It could be sticky love notes around the house or a nice massage. It could be absolutely everything that you know they will absolutely love. Something that will make them feel cared for.

PRINCIPLE #2: IT'S NOT A TRANSACTION

Never expect anything in return. It's your decision to implement this Skill, and this doesn't mean that your partner must do it as well. If you really want them to, you can pass them this book, and they'll decide for themselves. But until then, do your Weekly Surprise and expect nothing in return. It's not a transaction. You do it because you want to make sure that the person you love feels loved. You do it because you care and you want to make your relationship extraordinary.

HOW TO - SKILL #12

This Skill is as simple as it can get. All you need to do is make it happen once a week. It doesn't have to take you more than fifteen minutes. It doesn't have to be huge. But you must be consistent. I'll show you how to never forget to do it in the next STEP.

Once you start practicing The Weekly Surprise, you'll be amazed at yourself. Mostly, you'll be amazed at what a selfish jerk you've been up until now (that was my personal experience, at least). Staying true to this Skill will make sure that you never stop caring (for real). It will make sure that you are being a great partner at least once a week, every week (let's start small). You'll remind yourself of all the things that matter for the person you love. In the end, you'll most likely find yourself in a position where you receive much more love without asking for it (really, don't ask). Most importantly, you'll be with a better partner, because the person you are with will start blossoming around you and your greatness. It's a win-win, my friend. Let's start being great in our relationships!

SKILL #13: THE GAME PLAN

How do you go about planning your days and weeks? What is your guidebook?

If I come to your office or home and you let me open your phone or laptop and check your calendar, I'll be able to predict with a good amount of certainty what your chances are of succeeding and living a fulfilled life. Or more precisely, I'll be able to tell if you won't be able to succeed at all.

How? By seeing how you plan, what you plan, and if you plan at all. High-performing individuals are highly organized people. They plan their work. They plan their personal growth. They even plan their rest and leisure time. Of course, as with any rule, there ought to be exceptions, but I assure you, even the people who manage to succeed without great planning are leaving a lot of potential on the table.

I used to go without any plan in the early years of my career. Life was simple, and I was stupid. As time went by, my life started transforming into a complex net of responsibilities and tasks. I could no longer handle all of that. In the end, I crashed!

Sometimes you get to the bottom before you see the right path to the top. But you don't have to experience what I did to start planning much better and to start achieving superior results.

Several things I've observed are critical for everyone.

PRINCIPLE #1: WHAT, WHEN, WHY

We all have a stack of unfinished tasks and projects. Instead of getting overwhelmed, there is a pretty smart way to approach those to make sure we are in favor of maximum effectiveness.

In one of his videos, Tim Ferriss shares a set of questions that can help you prioritize your to-do list in a brilliant way. He suggests looking at your list and asking the following three questions:

"Which one of these, if accomplished, will make everything else easier or irrelevant?"
"Which of these, if checked off, will leave me satisfied with my day?"
"Which of these, if done, creates more time for me next week?"

By following his approach, I'm able to save a ton of time and make sure my focus stays on winning the game (long-term), instead of just keeping myself busy.

PRINCIPLE #2: HARD AND IMPORTANT FIRST

You might have heard about decision fatigue. If you haven't, it explains why we are more capable of making good decisions at the start and middle of our days compared with the end. Decision fatigue not only makes you less productive and creative but also carries a lot of stress.

This is one of the reasons why people like Mark Zuckerberg and Steve Jobs decided to wear the same type of outfit every day. Simply put, one less decision to make in the morning = one more decision at your disposal when most needed.

I've personally faced that issue, and it's not so much about the time of day, but rather the number of decisions you've been bombarded with. When I've experienced an extremely high load of questions from my team that required an immediate decision from my side, I could see my decision-making capability dropping to zero, sometimes even by midday.

Decision fatigue is not a myth. It's a reality that is connected with the way our brains are wired. So do what's most important when you are most productive and capable. Use your strongest hours to do what's hard and scary. Leave the simple tasks for the end of the day — email usually falls in there. This way, even if you only managed to achieve the top one or two important and difficult tasks for the day, you still kicked ass, and you can feel great.

And try to come up with some decisions you can take out of your daily menu. I haven't yet gone as extreme as Mark Zuckerberg, but I've decided to limit the types of clothing I wear. I have five white polo shirts and five navy blue polo shirts — all exactly the same model. I've done the same with my more formal shirts. It takes me a second to pick something, because they all match with my jeans, pants, and shoes. You can also make a meal plan for the whole month. Or build an IF-THEN decision-making process for simple questions. Whatever you come up with, try to eliminate some simple decisions and leave more space for what really matters.

PRINCIPLE #3: MY TOP 3 TASKS AND SKILLS

What are the top 3 tasks that will make your goals a reality? Once you are clear on those, you can break them down into smaller, actionable tasks and add them to your calendar.

What are the top 3 skills you need to practice and become great at to get to where you want to be in the next six months? Do the same here. Break them down, find the right mentors, and schedule practice hours in your calendar. These are your critical factors for success.

In racing, I needed to learn to do a few things really well to become a champion. I needed to be able to perform great in a single lap to beat the competition in qualifications. Then I needed to learn how to do several very quick laps at the start of each race to create a comfortable gap between myself and the person running in second place. And then I needed to be able to keep a consistent pace at about 95 percent of my best to keep the gap and prevent a mistake. So I had to practice differently to build up each skill and put it together during a racing weekend.

Most racing drivers used to spend a lot of time learning about the mechanics of the machines, which I knew absolutely nothing about — I still don't. They wasted valuable time reading heavy books and watching documentaries about the complex mechanical world of motorsport. But guess who knew everything about mechanics? My team of engineers did. And because I spent a lot of time on the track, I became great at feeling the machine and explaining its behavior to my engineers. Then they knew what changes needed to be made to fit my driving style and the conditions on the track. Other racing drivers and their teams might have been more knowledgeable by the book, but it was our team and our approach that won qualifications, races, and titles.

In our first business, our team needed to get solid partnerships with manufacturers and then SELL, SELL, SELL in the first years. Several years later, our company had more cash than anybody else but became massively disorganized, and we needed to focus on creating a sustainable structure for it. So we took a full year to implement software and processes. But we focused on what mattered most, depending on the circumstances. If we concentrated on structure in the first years, we would've died as a company in less than twelve months due to the lack of sufficient sales.

The Pareto Principle shows us how 80 percent of sales come from 20 percent of our clients, and 80 percent of results come from 20 percent of our effort. Figure out what this 20 percent is. Which are your 3 key tasks and 3 key skills that you need to focus on to reap maximum results? As much as possible, do more of those and less of the rest. What you do is extremely important. Very often, it's much more important than how much you do. Plan with this rule in your guidebook.

There's no excuse not to learn anything anymore. The Internet can teach you how to do absolutely everything these days. There's so much free value for the beginner levels, and there are hundreds of amazing online courses on literally any topic imaginable. Search for it, find it, learn it, apply it, teach someone else how to do it. In a matter of months, you can go from zero to hero in so many areas.

And always remind yourself of the major goal and the reason behind it and reverse-engineer from there. I know many knowledgeable and skillful people who achieve next to nothing because they are lost in randomness. Know and do the right stuff that will get you where you want to go!

PRINCIPLE #4: LESS IS MORE

What are your daily tasks? Which of those can you automate completely or at least to a certain extent?

I'll give you one: email. Maybe you can't automate it entirely, but you certainly write repetitive emails every now and then. We all do. You can create templates that have 95 percent of the information prefilled. This way, all you need to do to send this email again is load the template and fill in the other 5 percent. It might save you a minute a day. It might save you an hour. It depends on your email game. But it only takes a few minutes to create those templates that will save you some precious hours every year. And that's only from email.

You can also automate certain orders by subscribing for monthly deliveries. You can automate text message responses, credit card, and bill payments, social media posts, filling online forms, digital backups (phone and computer), regular communication with clients, and more.

What else can we do?

Here's an even more exciting one. How much is a strong hour of your work worth? How much are you getting paid, or how much does your best-invested hour of work earn your company? How much do you want your hour to be worth, depending on the lifestyle you want to build? How can you increase its worth? By adding more value.

How do you add more value? By being more creative and delivering better results. And in most cases, you do this by investing extra time. But we don't want to spend our lives working, right? We want this new lifestyle. We want to find the right balance and still be able to achieve a lot in every area.

The answer is: we delegate.

It doesn't matter whether you are a CEO of a large corporation, a young entrepreneur who's just starting off, or a great employee who wants to grow in their career. There is much you can delegate to be more effective, more productive, and to make your hours worth much more.

Today there are endless opportunities for delegation. Some are extremely cheap and at the same time add great quality.

Think for a second. Which of your daily tasks take a lot of time and can be done by someone else? If you don't know how much time you spend on each task, time it. Many mobile apps will help you do that. I've personally used Hours Time Tracking and Toggl. Both get the job done.

Some tasks you might want to consider delegating are grocery delivery, cooking, cleaning, distribution, marketing, editing, transcribing, research, data entry, accounting, legal, and driving.

Basically, anything that is repetitive, streamlined, and is not part of your core work. In some cases, it's also a great idea to delegate things you simply dislike doing.

For many tasks that can be delegated digitally, you can use apps like UpWork, Fiverr, and other Virtual Assistant services. Before you delegate, make sure you create a very clear guideline (in writing) for the person who will be taking over the work. Hold daily, then weekly meetings to make sure that the person is perfectly clear with his/her task. When you see that they are doing the job as assigned, give them some more freedom, while staying involved, and pour all the extra hours into what matters most to you and your Mission.

So what are your three tasks to automate and three tasks to delegate? Test it out and see how much time you can save.

HOW TO - SKILL #13

Many people plan the day the night before. But we'll take a different approach here. Day planning is too shortsighted. We want to plan the whole week ahead (at a designated time every week), since it is a full week in which we'll be able to practice each of our Skills. We can always make adjustments for each day throughout the week, but we want to have a broader vision and plan that includes everything meaningful before we have started the new week. Don't worry about it yet, since our next STEP is all about planning.

Remember your SMURT Goals? They will be the goals that will drive all of your weekly planning. No more thinking small, my friend. It's time to get to work and kick some serious ass. Trust me! You've never had so much fun.

SKILL #14: THE FINANCIAL FREEDOM

I opened my bank account for the first time in over six months. Not that I really cared about what was going on in there, but out of curiosity. I was making more than $30,000 per month already, so I knew I didn't need to worry about money.

Or did I?

My bank account balance shocked me. I thought there was a mistake, so I *gently* hit "Refresh" several times. But the number was still the same: just over $400. I didn't have any other accounts. I didn't have any cash or any investments other than my business. That was all the money I had.

"Where the f*ck is my money!?" I was starting to sweat.

I began digging through the monthly transactions to see what the hell happened to all the money I was supposed to have. An hour later, I gave up. Unfortunately, there was no mistake.

I HAD SPENT IT ALL!

I was starting to feel wealthy and thought that my money problems were gone. So I began racing as a hobby, and I crashed several times, one of which was an ugly head-on rally crash into a tree. I had to pay some big sums for repairs. Then I got a huge apartment, I was spending a considerable amount on alcohol, I was flying business class, I was sleeping in the most expensive hotels.

And while all that might sound like fun, I realized if anything happened to my business tomorrow, I was broke. With all the fixed expenses I had (apartment, car, food, etc.), I was going to go underwater in less than a month. And what about the future? What if I was forced to retire one day?

I quickly came to realize that it's not just about how much money you make but also about how much money you get to keep (invest). A guy who makes $100,000 and spends that same amount every year will eventually be poorer and in much more trouble than a girl who makes $10,000 and invests 10 percent of that in assets every year.

But I feared investing in anything other than my business. It was "too risky" for me. I had no control. "What if I invest 10 percent of my monthly income and it goes down the drain? It will feel terrible to lose that money."

I decided to sit and think over that problem, which was starting to make me seriously nervous. My thoughts went something like this:

On one hand, I can invest that money and take some risk for a large potential long-term gain. On the other hand, I can spend it on more stuff, a bigger apartment, more expensive hotels, a nicer TV, a few more pairs of jeans, and an expensive wristwatch.

Wait a minute…

If I don't invest that 10 percent every month, the risk of losing it is 100 percent. The minute I buy any of those things, the money is gone. And even if I don't spend that money and just let it sit there in my checking or savings account, the 2-3 percent inflation rate will eat it up. And let's be honest, I'll spend it all anyway!

By investing, at least I have a chance of profiting. And even if I do make a mistake in the beginning, I'll gain experience and make smarter choices later. Eventually, I'll get better in that game, and I'll be able to minimize the risks and increase the upside opportunities.

What an idiot!

When I realized I was losing by default by fearing investing, I started reading about it and learning what I needed to do.

The only major problem I had was my mindset (that's one hell of a problem to have). I might have learned how to make good money through my business, but I was still thinking like a person who was barely making ends meet.

Think about that for a second. How would you feel if you never had to worry about student loans, or your mortgage, car payments, utilities, bills, food, university costs for your kids? How would you feel if you only worked because you wanted to and not because you had to?

That is what I wanted to achieve for myself, and that is what I want you to achieve too. A life where you won't be a prisoner of money.

Here's what I learned.

PRINCIPLE #1: LIVE LONG AND HAPPILY

People with a rich mindset know that generating cash is not enough. They know that once they retire (if they want to) they'll need a significant amount of money (passive income) to be able to sustain the lifestyle they were able to build in their most active years. That's a lot of money, bearing in mind that some people live to over a hundred years. People who know how to play the game make long-term investments.

PRINCIPLE #2: OWN MORE, CONSUME LESS

We are great consumers, but most of us never invest in becoming owners. We buy an iPhone for $1,000, but we own $0 of Apple stock. This mentality is what makes and keeps us poor our whole lives. I don't say invest in Apple stock or don't buy the new iPhone. I say that a person with a rich mentality is more of an owner and less of a consumer.

Simply spend less than you earn and invest the surplus. A shinier car won't make you feel more secure, trust me. A bigger house or apartment won't either. Been there. Doesn't work. There's no need to impress anyone. Not with material stuff anyways. You are not your car or your wristwatch.

Don't fall into this trap. Always live below your means. If you are making $30,000, live like you are making $25,000. Why? Why would you wait to get all these things you want so badly? The answer is: because you are not there yet. And there's nothing wrong with that. You'll get there sooner if you play smart. But if you jump in and spend all your money on stuff that doesn't help you increase your future gains, in the best-case scenario, you will be stuck in the same place forever.

So instead of using up all the cash on luxuries that will bring you super short-term satisfaction, invest that money in your future. Invest it in owning more assets instead of being just another consumer.

This is the only way to join the 0.1% who get richer with time.

And don't get me wrong. I do believe you must get many of the material things you want. Not because they'll make you feel amazing, but because you'll realize that after a certain level, where you have a great home, a nice, comfortable car, and you can travel the world and experience the things you love, those material things add absolutely no value to your life experience. In fact, they make you a prisoner who must generate a certain amount of cash only to be able to keep up with that new standard, instead of setting yourself free so you can do what you love the most and live life on your own terms.

PRINCIPLE #3: WHERE IS THE MONEY?

But how do you find extra money to invest if you are already spending everything you earn?

For most of us, that's pretty simple. Do you have the new iPhone or Samsung Galaxy? Or maybe the Google Pixel? How much did you spend on shoes this year?

Much of the world complains that they lack the resources to start a business and follow their dreams. Yet they carry $2,000 worth of branded products around every day and have a few grand more gathering dust at home. The mere price of a phone like that ($1,000) is enough for you to set up a corporation, start a website, buy your first products, and invest over $500 in marketing for your first sale. Are you still sure you don't have the money?

If you don't spend big lump sums on such products, and you are still not sure how you can save 10 percent a month, do the following: make a list of all your monthly expenses and group them by type (rent, utilities, cars, insurance, eating out, groceries, etc.) You can use an app by Intuit called Mint that does this automatically for you. Look through the groups, especially the big ones. What can you cut down on that won't affect the quality of your life?

Last week I turned thirty. We went out with friends for dinner, and in a typical Bulgarian style, I paid the check in the end. It was the cheapest birthday I've ever had, even though I was now living in Los Angeles, which is about twice as expensive as Sofia,

Bulgaria. How come? We went to a very nice restaurant in Malibu, and we ate some amazing and quite pricey food.

The answer was very simple: nobody drank any alcohol. My wife and I stopped drinking more than two years ago (except a glass or two on rare occasions). I decided to estimate the savings we made from that simple habit change.

Let's say we drink three times a week, and we both have two glasses of red wine, which cost $10 per glass. I used to drink much more than that, but let's be conservative for the sake of this example.

Here's the simple math:

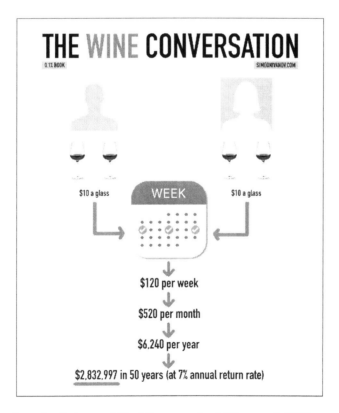

2 people x 2 glasses x $10 x 3 times a week = $120 per week / $520 per month / $6,240 per year

And even though these two glasses of wine might not sound like such a huge deal, if we were to invest the savings ($520 per month) in an account with an assumed 7% annual return rate (which is quite normal in the long term), they would have hypothetically turned into $2,832,997 in 50 years when we retire.

Did I just ruin red wine for you?

I don't suggest that you ditch your two glasses of wine. I didn't stop drinking alcohol to save money. I stopped because I knew it didn't help me perform at my best. But I did stop many stupid subscriptions, and I stopped purchasing products that I didn't need. I also sold many of the things that were just lying around at home without any great purpose.

Currently, I'm in the process of eliminating bottled water from our household; we used to spend over $200 per month on it (not a typo, and yes, I know how stupid this is). Instead, we'll buy a water purifier and use water from the tap. The saved $200 will automatically be added to long-term investments.

Do the math and see where you are making silly decisions instead of saving and investing for the things that you really want.

PRINCIPLE #4: THE SOONER, THE BETTER

Albert Einstein said: "Compound interest is the eighth wonder of the world. He who understands it, earns it. He who doesn't, pays it."

Taking advantage of compound interest is key to generating bigger returns. What is compound interest? I'll borrow an explanation from Investopedia.com to make sure I don't confuse anyone with my amateur street talk.

"Compound interest (or compounding interest) is interest calculated on the initial principal and also on the accumulated interest of previous period of a deposit or loan. Compound interest can be thought of as 'interest on interest,' and will make a sum grow at a faster rate than simple interest, which is calculated only on the principal amount."

Let me give you a real-world example that people like me will find easier to get.

Let's say I invest $10,000 at the age of thirty and keep it till I'm seventy in a compound interest account with an assumed 7 percent annual return (this is calculated to be the average for the S&P 500 index between 1950 and 2009). By the end of the period, my balance has grown to $163,114.

But what if I started ten years earlier? So I kept my investments of $10,000 for a total of fifty years at the same 7 percent annual rate. The end result is $327,804. I've made double the amount by starting ten years earlier. I could have also achieved the same hypothetical result of $163,114 by investing much less money ($4,976 to be exact) than in the previous example.

So here's how passing on an extra Starbucks cup of coffee, or a glass of wine, or maybe bottled water can make a big difference due to the power of compounding. Check this table and do the math for yourself. How can you start saving five, ten, fifteen dollars a day so you'll have extra money to invest? The difference this could make for your life by the time you need to retire could be colossal.

DAILY SAVINGS	MONTHLY INVESTMENT	10 YEARS	20 YEARS	30 YEARS	40 YEARS	50 YEARS
$5	$150	$25,693	$78,139	$182,996	$393,722	$817,211
$10	$300	$51,925	$156,278	$365,991	$787,444	$1,634,421
$15	$450	$77,888	$234,417	$548,987	$1,181,166	$2,451,632
$20	$600	$103,851	$312,556	$731,983	$1,574,888	$3,268,843
$30	$900	$155,776	$468,834	$1,097,974	$2,362,332	$4,903,464
$40	$1,200	$207,702	$625,112	$1,463,965	$3,149,776	$6,537,685
$50	$1,500	$259,627	$781,390	$1,829,956	$3,937,220	$8,172,106
$100	$3,000	$519,254	$1,562,780	$3,659,913	$7,874,440	$16,355,213

THE POWER OF COMPOUNDING (Assumes 7% Annual Rate of Return)

PRINCIPLE #5: LONG-TERM PLAYERS WIN

I'm not a fan of gambling. Therefore, I'm not a fan of active trading (buying and selling stocks or other investments on a regular basis). The last time I tried to figure out the movement between EUR/USD, I saw how for six months, 90 percent of the so-called experts were giving the exact opposite advice from what followed as a market movement. It almost made sense to read their projections and do the exact opposite if you wanted to succeed (don't do that, by the way).

So I prefer not to play the game of market timing and day-trading. I want to focus on what I'm great at and leave the money to work for me in the long term and compound automatically.

Warren Buffett said:

"We've long felt that the only value of stock forecasters is to

make fortune tellers look good. Even now, Charlie and I continue
to believe that short-term market forecasts are poison and should
be kept locked up in a safe place, away from children and also
from grown-ups who behave in the market like children ... Some
things just take time: You can't produce a baby in one month by
getting nine women pregnant. If you aren't willing to own a stock
for ten years, don't even think about owning it for ten minutes."

So all I've done is set up a widely diversified investment
portfolio, and a portion of my income goes there automatically
every month without me even seeing that money. I invest a little
more every month, and the plan is that I won't sell until it's time to
retire (if I ever retire). When the markets go down (which they
inevitably will, as we've seen from history), I'll have some savings
and will be happy to invest some more and buy cheap.

Is this the best thing to do? I don't know. I'm far from an expert
in this field. But I'm trying to learn from history and from the
experts, and I know that if I don't invest anything, the chances that
I will end up broke one day increase significantly. I prefer taking a
little risk.

If you are new to investing, I recommend you read the
following three books, in this order:

Rich Dad Poor Dad by Robert Kiyosaki
I Will Teach You to Be Rich by Ramit Sethi
Money: Master the Game by Tony Robbins

Once you learn the basics, you can get yourself a copy of the
Series 7 Exam Course Textbook and dive a bit deeper by learning
the same things that licensed stockbrokers have to learn at the start
of their careers. I did that, and it was helpful, but I don't think it's
necessary for anyone, because it won't add much more value than

the books I already mentioned, which are written in plain English that is accessible to all of us.

You don't need to be an expert to start investing. But you do need to start investing to secure your financial future.

HOW TO – SKILL #14

Please, note that all that I'm sharing here is my personal opinion (and what I do) and is in no way a recommendation for how you must handle your money. I'm not an expert, and I strongly believe that before you make any decision, you must seek duly licensed professional investment advice. Use my writings for information purposes only. Investing always holds risks, as I've mentioned above, and you can win but also lose all the money that you've invested.

With that said, here's my opinion of what you must do to practice this Skill.

1) SET A GOAL

Until you read the three books I mentioned and you are ready to set up an automated investment system for your money game, I want you to think of a single goal now.

Do you have debt you need to pay off?

Do you have enough savings in case of emergencies (three to six months of your total expenses)?

Do you need to save for university, your wedding, your first home?

Or do you want to start a business and need extra cash?

Pick your most important goal and write it down.

2) FIND THE BEST SAVINGS ACCOUNT

Go to your calendar and include a one-hour Success Block that will be dedicated to finding and comparing the best savings accounts you have access to. Look for one with no set-up and monthly fees and with a high-interest return. Also, make sure that the accounts in this bank have deposit insurance by the government. In the United States, such deposits are insured up to $250,000 per account owner, so you won't have to worry that the bank might go bust.

3) SET IT UP

When you have found the best savings account (probably through an online bank), you can set up a free account. This should take no longer than ten minutes. Name this account (most accounts allow you to add a nickname) with the name of the goal you are trying to achieve. So your account can be named "Three-Month Safety Net" or "Debt Free, Baby!" Whatever makes you feel great about that goal.

4) AUTOMATE

Then you can go to your checking account at your primary bank (where your paycheck goes) and set up an automatic monthly transfer to your new savings account that represents 10 percent of your current monthly income. Make sure you pay no fees for the auto transfers between the two accounts. This means that you will not have to do anything, and each month this sum will be automatically transferred from your checking to your high-yield savings account, where it will start growing and compounding.

Even though savings accounts today offer minimal interest returns (except in some countries), it is the best first step before you inform yourself about the world of investing and take the next important step. It will help you prioritize your expenses and start living below your means from tomorrow.

When you are ready to move to the next step and open an

investment account, you will have money saved up in your savings account that you can easily transfer.

Every week in which your automated system worked, and you saved and/or invested your planned amount, you accomplished your Skill, and you can pat yourself on the back for this small but important win.

When I realized I'd been ruining my money game, when I started taking the right actions, when I implemented this Skill and started leveling up from cutting off on silly spending to saving and investing … well, I managed to live off of my savings for over a year without making a single dollar. That allowed me to write this book without having to worry about the bills. And that, my friend, is worth the world to me.

There is no investment without risk. Whatever you invest in, you can lose some or all of your money. But that holds true for keeping your money under your pillow or at a checking account in the bank. And that's even truer if you spend it on stuff you don't need.

SKILL #15: THE SECRET MASTERMIND

My brother and my nephew went to the playground in the park. The little guy had just learned to walk a few months earlier and was still afraid to play on the slides. They must have looked high and dangerous to him. My brother tried showing him how it's done, but my nephew refused to go by himself. Then a few other kids that were a little older than him joined. They started sliding, one after the other. Guess what my nephew did a few minutes later? He was pushing through the older kids to slide. And he did it over, and over, and over again. No fear. Just pure joy.

Why? Why didn't he do it by himself or when my brother showed him? Because he never saw anyone else who looked as little as himself do it. He saw his father as an adult. He's different. He can talk. He's big. But once he saw the other kids slide, he knew he could easily do it too. They were not special or different. They were just like him.

Are you surrounded by peers who know how to handle the big slides? Can they do things that you still can't or things that you are afraid of? Do they want to learn and grow? Are they open to sharing and supporting you?

Becoming a part of a group where you feel inspired and supported is a must if you want to explore the heights of your potential and join the Club of the 0.1%. If you still don't have a Mastermind group of three, four, five people who regularly gather (or do conference calls) and strategically discuss how they can support each other in achieving their Missions, you are missing out on a ton of opportunities.

Note that these people don't need to be your childhood friends or family. If you don't receive this support and motivation from your lifelong friends, that doesn't mean you need to stop communicating with them. It means that you need to have a separate group that gives you that. It means that you need to plan how much time you'll be investing in each group, depending on what you're trying to achieve in your life.

Never push your friends to become like you. Give them the best personal example possible. Inspire them. They'll follow your steps if they want to and when they feel ready. You can't change them. Only they can do that for themselves.

PRINCIPLE #1: FINDING THE RIGHT PEOPLE

What are the best places to find highly motivated, hard-working individuals with high aspirations in life? People that might be a great addition to your Secret Mastermind group. This obviously depends on the industry your Mission is targeting, but you cannot go wrong by attending professional and personal development seminars or volunteering groups.

PRINCIPLE #2: START GROWING TODAY

If you still can't find the people who inspire you and who pull you closer to your best self, don't worry. You can start learning from the best in the world right now.

When I started paying more attention to my personal and professional growth, I started researching who the best experts in the world are for each field of interest. I read their books. I listened to and watched all their free content. I bought many of their online courses and went to their seminars.

I remember buying my first expensive online course from Brendon Burchard several years ago. Brendon is a high-performance expert, a marketing ninja, and an extremely smart and funny guy. He's also one of the most generous people in the self-help industry, so I trusted him. The course was $2,000, which seemed a lot to me at that time. But it had a thirty-day money-back guarantee, so I thought I'd give it a shot. In the first couple of hours of the four-week course, I was confident that I got a return on my investment and much more above that. By the end of it, I knew I'd saved hundreds of thousands, if not millions of dollars by taking the course (no exaggeration; I'd never met Brendon, and I'm not paid to say that). I've saved myself expensive mistakes and a ton of time. I've also found strategies I could literally copy and paste that would later significantly increase the impact of my Mission.

Now, Brendon and other experts have courses from which I didn't get as much value, but other people did. You only need to find one thing that will make that crucial difference for you. But for that to happen, you need to invest. Some people spend $2,000 on a new TV screen. I prefer to spend it on courses and learn shoulder to shoulder with the best in each field. Invest in learning from those who've already been where you want to get. The benefits often exceed the cost.

When you are researching experts online, you need to be careful. Beware of fake influencers. There are thousands of people who are faking their popularity and influence. One way to know if that's the case is to use socialblade.com. This website shows you the growth charts of followers for everyone's social media accounts. For example, if you see that an "expert" follows and unfollows hundreds of people on Instagram every day, it means he/she is using bots to gain more followers — he/she is faking it. If you see that someone has gained thousands of followers in one day but loses followers on a daily basis — he/she is faking it.

I've found that to be a great tool to see whether someone is real and honest or is just trying to bullshit us into believing he is followed and respected by clients.

Don't let yourself be fooled by dishonest people. Do your research before spending your sweet money.

PRINCIPLE #3: SETTING UP THE GROUP

If you start growing today in the fields you are interested in, soon enough you won't need to search for people to join your Mastermind group. Why? Because the more you expand your knowledge and influence, the more other inspired and great people will want to work with you.

Remember that at the beginning of this book I asked you to find two friends with whom to share the experience? If they also have gone through all of the exercises so far, they can surely become your first two Mastermind members.

All you need to do is talk to them and set up a monthly two-hour meeting. In those meetings, each member of the group will get the same amount of time to share your goals, your progress, and the support/advice you need to be able to move forward faster. After each of you is done sharing, the other members give their feedback, their suggestions, and propose how they can help (if they can).

HOW TO – SKILL #15

Other than the monthly Mastermind meetings, you will also create several chat groups (one for each member) inviting all members in each group. You can use WhatsApp, Telegram, Viber, or another similar app for the purpose. One of the chat groups will be named after you, and the rest of the groups will be named after each of the other members. In every group, you will be sharing your personal Skill performance and progress by the end of every single day.

When the day is over, I make screenshots of my Skill performance (I'll show you how in the next STEP), and I send those to chat group, "Simeon 0.1%" where everybody else can see them. If my performance sucks, other members must get in touch and help me improve the next day.

Each of these groups is dedicated solely to sharing and discussing your growth and nothing else. No dog pictures and no jokes. That goes into your everyday communication, which is separate.

This is one of the most important Skills of the system because it expands the responsibility from just yourself to a group of like-minded, motivated people who are seeking to be their best, just like you.

When you are in a Mastermind group, you are responsible for your growth as much as everybody else's. If you grow, you will be able to help others grow. You'll give a great example. If you help your group members grow, they will be able to help you grow even more. It works just like compound interest.

If you initially find no one to practice this Skill with, you can make screenshots and post your Skill performance on Instagram or Facebook and tag @0.1book or @simeonivanov (I'll tell you how to do that in the next STEP). I'll post my own performance in this page every day as a "Story," and I'll do my best to check yours out and see if you need any guidance.

Know that no matter how smart you are, you are much smarter when a few more brains are working toward your growth in every important area of your life. You cannot beat that alone.

My Secret Mastermind is constantly helping me to avoid costly mistakes and to see opportunities that are out of my sight. It breathes a significant amount of extra energy and brain power into everything I do. It makes me a better learner, a better leader, a better human being.

14

THE RIPPLE EFFECT

Six months into practicing the Big Fifteen Skills…

The pupils of their eyes expanded rapidly. They looked at the car, then looked back at my brother and me. They were shocked. I could see a hint of warm tears building up in their eyes and pushing through for their freedom. I didn't remember the last time I saw my mom and dad cry happy tears.

It was my dad's birthday.

We passed him the keys to his brand-new, shiny black Mercedes S63 AMG, which we thought was a good fit for him since he was born in 1963.

My brother encouraged him to sit in the driver's seat, but my dad just stayed there for some time. He had no words, and neither did my mom.

We thought that he would be super excited about the car. We knew how much he loved cars. Especially fast ones. But it wasn't so much the car that made him that happy. It was the gesture and the fact that his two sons managed to afford such a birthday present for their father while still in their twenties.

He couldn't hide his pure, fatherly pride that was burning stronger than the August sun.

After a very long pause, he finally went for it and sat behind the steering wheel. "So, do you like it?" I asked him. In response, he pushed the throttle to the steel plate. The 577-horsepower engine roared like a wild beast. Our dad looked at us and through laughter and tears said, "I love this game!"

We left the car and went in for dinner at the restaurant.

Halfway through the celebration, I was laughing so much that my whole body flushed with warm blood and I needed to stand up and take off my jacket. I couldn't help but notice that many of the women from the surrounding tables in front of me stopped talking and eating and just stared at me.

What the hell? I thought.

I started checking myself out to see whether I had spilled sauce on my shirt. But there was no stain. They were checking *me* out. They were checking the results of six months of strategic, deliberate, hard work. This was the first time I felt the silent but obvious appreciation of my little experiment. And I won't hide it — it felt great!

And it wasn't just these women. Everyone at our table was acting differently toward me. They were treating me with a different level of respect. They were more interested in what I had to say. My dad even asked me, "How can you always be so happy?"

What nobody seemed to remember is that I wasn't "always" so happy. It's just that people (even your family) remember you for the way you've been in the past couple of months.

In fact, a year earlier, I was in a deep depression and happiness was not a word that existed in my dictionary.

But now I was excited about life all the time. I had so much energy. I was working out, meditating, reading, eating healthy, sleeping well. I was organized and was taking action like a warrior. Our company's results skyrocketed. I was crushing the game at work and in my personal life.

"Damn, life's amazing!" That's how I felt almost all of the time.

My system was working! And everything that I was doing, every small Skill that I was practicing, was generating a massive ripple effect throughout every important area of my life.

In six months, I transformed all fields I valued. I never felt so great in my life. I looked much better than ever before. I was making much more money and making much smarter decisions about it than ever before. I was able to care more for the people I loved. I learned how to celebrate every day of my life for the first time.

With this level of vitality, confidence, and excitement, I knew I was on my way to creating all the things I wanted to experience in life. And it seemed that everyone around me was feeling that energy too. And you know what? They all wanted to know how. They all wanted the magic pill.

But you already know the secret. There's no magic pill. It's the power of the Big Fifteen Skills and the Ripple Effect that we create by practicing them all at the same time.

THE "SECRET"

Think what will happen if you did your best to improve your sleep, and you practiced only Skill #1: The Sweet Dreams without any of the other Skills. Yes, your sleep might improve a little. But if the quality of your life sucks and you are stressed-out and unfulfilled in your personal and work life, you probably won't have a great night of sleep either.

On the other hand, if you did practice all the Skills every week, you would be moving the whole scale more toward the 0.1% and away from the 99.9%. If you knew that you are doing your best to improve every important area of your life and you were already seeing significant results, wouldn't that help you have the best sleep ever? Wouldn't you feel calmer, happier, much more satisfied? Of course you would.

You see, it is a mistake to try to focus on a single area or a single Skill, because our success at every Skill is closely linked to our success at all other Skills and ultimately to the quality of our lives.

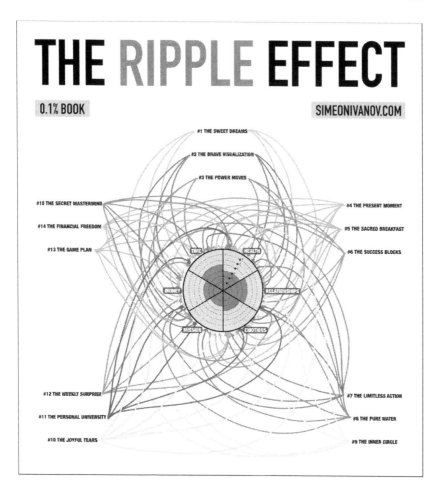

You might be thinking that mastering Skill #6: The Success Blocks will do wonders for your Mission and Money fields, but you will come to realize that it also has a tremendous impact on your Emotions, your Relationships, your Health, and even your Time field. And that holds true for all the other Skills that you'll implement in your system.

Every single Skill that you will begin practicing creates a Ripple Effect throughout all areas of your life. And this Ripple Effect is what will bring you the results you seek much faster. It is what makes this system so powerful.

These are the basic Skills you need to achieve a massive transformation in every important area of your life. Now, let me show you how to implement them in your system so that you can become as disciplined as a US Navy SEAL. It'll be as simple and as fun as playing a video game — only much more rewarding.

Are you ready?

Let's do it!

STEP IV: THE METHOD

THE POWER OF ROUTINE

"You must methodize your life. God created routine. The sun shines until dusk and the stars shine until dawn."

— Paramahansa Yogananda

Remember the first time you drove a car? I certainly remember mine. Even though I was already a racing driver, I was scared as shit! I didn't know what I needed to do — there was just too much. I had to accelerate, shift gears (yep, manual gears), look in all three mirrors, brake on time, look at all the road signs, the pedestrians, signal for turning, find the damn windshield wipers… It was a huge mess. And then on top of all that, I needed to get from point A to point B, and I really sucked at remembering the right way around the city. By the time I was done with my first thirty-minute drive, I was already soaking wet and mentally destroyed. I just wanted to go to sleep and never have to drive again.

A few months later, I was driving with one hand, listening to music, talking with friends. Whenever I reached a destination, I didn't even remember that I drove. *How the hell did I get here? Did I drive?*

That's exactly what will start happening with the Skills and your life. In the first couple of days, you might suck, just as I did. That's normal. Don't beat yourself up. But when you keep on using the system, when you show up every day, eventually you will start rocking this game. You will become a beast (if that's what you want)! Let me rephrase. You will finally start experiencing life the way you have always wanted to. You will start living in a flow state of being. You will start performing at a top level. You will start getting bigger results in every area. You will love it!

It's not about whether we do the easy or difficult. It's about whether we do the right (important) or the wrong (unimportant) things. What you are about to learn now will make you a master at always doing what's right.

You must think big and start small. Small wins add up and ultimately make you great.

15

START OVER

"I've made it!"

I had everything I ever wanted in my life. I had my favorite car. The apartment I was dreaming of. The business that was helping save people's lives and was making millions of dollars. I had everything everybody else wanted to have. Everybody told me how successful I was. But … I've never felt worse than that in my life.

There was a huge emptiness in my heart. An emptiness that wouldn't disappear. I bought all the stuff I thought I must buy to make myself happy. I even went back to racing eight years after I quit, spending hundreds of thousands of dollars — I thought that that would light the spark in my soul again. But … no. That was not the answer either.

I could see how everybody else around me was playing that same game. A game we could never win. We were all buying useless stuff to fill the emptiness. We were spending our hard-earned money on bullshit. We were seeking experiences to make ourselves feel good. We were going into relationships that were destined for failure before they had even begun. We were all running after the next promotion, the next paycheck, the next gadget, the next vacation ... seeking what? Happiness?

How do you go on a journey to search for something before you have taken the time to understand what it really is? How do you find something when you are searching for it in a place where it can never be found? How do you think you'll figure out what this thing is for you, while still wearing a hundred pairs of glasses — other people's opinions?

We were all running on a messed-up autopilot that was destroying our lives. This autopilot wasn't designed to do us any good. It was designed to keep us small and miserable. It was designed to keep us safe and protected but was instead leading to fear and premature death — the death of our souls.

I realized I needed to take a massive step back. I needed to take a fresh look, forgetting about what society told me life was about. I needed to stop believing even my own thoughts about what was good, what was possible, and what would make me happy. I'd been programmed the wrong way for far too long. I needed to listen to my intuition. I needed to strategize, test, create an action plan, and go for it without looking back.

It was a Saturday morning, and I was about to do my usual weekly planning session at home. I turned my laptop on, and while waiting for it to load, I looked at the beautiful view outside. It was a sunny day, but I could barely feel that because of the dark walls and furniture in my apartment. I felt like going out, but I knew I needed to plan. So I planned. But this time, instead of planning for an hour, I was going to plan all day. And instead of planning the work week ahead, I was going to plan how I wanted my life to continue.

If I were to die tomorrow, next week, next month, next year, what must I do every day to make sure my life was worth living?

When I woke up the next day, I marked something in my calendar (exactly twelve months ahead). It was the day my life was to start over. But this time, the way I wanted it. I was to sell my business and decide what I was going to do and where I was going to do it by that date. I was to leave my country and all the comforts that I'd been creating for the past decades of my life. I was to burn every single boat and start over — leaving the past where it belonged. I was to design my life for success and excitement — not the way everybody else was telling me I should.

...

I leaned back in my seat, feeling happier than ever before. I closed my eyes and felt the wheels of the airplane lifting off the ground, the same way all my pain had lifted off my chest in the past several months. I checked my Google Calendar before I put my phone in airplane mode. It looked weird. I hadn't seen it empty for a long time. The whole week was just blank space except for one single note. It was that note I scheduled for this day, exactly twelve months ago. It was a bold note, a bold promise I made to myself: *Start over!*

It was time!

My friend, nobody cares if you messed up yesterday, last week, last month, or the last ten years of your life. And you shouldn't either. Learn from your mistakes and start over today! This moment is all there really is. You have full control over what you are going to do with your life.

16

METHODIZE, METHODIZE, METHODIZE

WINNING

I looked at my watch. It was 1:30 p.m. Exactly thirty minutes before the start of the race. I knew exactly what I needed to do.

Without any hesitation, I went to the team's office, locked myself up in the quiet room, and started my visualization. I closed my eyes and suddenly found myself strapped in the cockpit, on the grid, waiting for the lights to come off ... 3 ... 2 ... 1 ... GO! GO! GO! I was holding the throttle at about 90 percent and released the clutch with the precision of a world-class neurosurgeon. The rear wheels started drifting, but just enough to propel me forward in a perfect fashion. I overtook two of my rivals and went on to complete the perfect first lap of the race. Just as I crossed the finish line in this first lap, I opened my eyes.

I looked at my watch. It was 1:35 p.m. I knew exactly what I needed to do next.

I started putting my racing suit on. I would always do it in the same exact sequence. I would put my fireproof underwear first, starting with the socks, then the bottom and finally the top. Then it was time for the racing suit. Finally, I would put my racing shoes on. Then it was time to prepare my helmet and check if everything was in place: gloves (check), bonnet (check), Hans device (check).

I looked at my watch. It was 1:40 p.m. I knew exactly what I needed to do next.

I went into the pit and put my helmet on the formula. It was time for my warmup. As usual, I did exactly two minutes of stretching, sixty jumping jacks, thirty seconds of high-knees, and twenty pushups. Why this number? Because I knew that by finishing this ritual at about fifteen minutes before the race, my heart rate would be at its perfect range for me to be able to react the fastest when the red lights went off. I knew that because the team at Formula Medicine tested my reactions with computers in a hundred different circumstances. This warmup worked like magic.

I looked at my watch. It was 1:45 p.m. I sat in the cockpit of the formula and my engineer fastened the six seatbelts as tight as possible. Now it was all up to me. I knew exactly what I needed to do next. I was going to have another perfect race start!

It must have been 2:00 p.m. sharp, because all formulas were now lined on the grid. The lights went off, and I did what I knew best. I was holding the throttle at about 90 percent and released the clutch with the precision of a world-class neurosurgeon. The rear wheels started drifting, but just enough to propel me forward in a perfect fashion.

Ten seconds after the start of the race, I was already two places ahead.

I'd always been one of the fastest racing drivers in starts. Why? Was it because I was more talented or had more experience? No. Neither of these was really the case. The only reality was this: I was extremely diligent in following my tested and proven routine, while most other racing drivers weren't.

LOSING

I taught one of my best friends from Miami (let's call him Bryan) to use the system. I helped him set up The Method, and he started working on The Skills.

He was going through a lot of shit in his life. But not because life gave him shit. He was creating it through his lifestyle. His diet consisted of 50 percent junk food. He was extremely stressed out about his work life, even though he was making a lot of money and business was going very well. He was smoking weed every day, saying that it "helped him relax" after a stressful day at work. He didn't drink more than a liter of water a day but "supplemented" with several coffees instead. He didn't read, didn't work out, didn't spend quality time with his family and friends. It is safe to say he didn't really live.

I got seriously scared for him and wanted to help. I was lucky (and he was even luckier) that he wanted to be helped as well and was ready to receive the lessons and do the work.

I really hoped that he would start using the system. I knew that if it helped him recover and flourish, it would do wonders for anyone.

So he did. We worked on the exact same Skills that I shared with you in the previous STEP. I also added him to my personal Secret Mastermind where we shared our progress with each other every day.

In just a single week, Bryan was himself again. Even more, he was a better version of himself, one that we never knew existed. He was feeling energized, enthusiastic about life, happy.

A few weeks later, he was already losing a significant amount of fat weight, his lungs were clearing up, and he was inventing some extraordinary new possibilities to grow his business. Even more, he was taking serious action and was making things happen. He also said that it was the first time since he started the business that he hadn't shouted at work.

Oh, I almost forgot to tell you this. Before he started using the system, Bryan was stuttering so badly, it would sometimes take him ten seconds to say a single word. Now, the stutter was almost gone. Why? Because he was feeling fulfilled. He was relaxed. He was f*cking happy.

Bryan got ripped in less than a year (the bastard looked much better than me). He was more energetic and happier than ever. His business was hitting unexpectedly high volumes of sales and profits. His personal and family life got better than ever before.

So, just like most of us do when everything is going great, Bryan stopped using the system. And it was my fault that I didn't do much about it. Since we didn't live close to each other, I didn't see him for almost a year. When I did saw him (one year after he stopped), things didn't look pretty.

Bryan never looked so bad in his life. He was getting fat, he was smoking again, he hadn't worked out for a year and didn't practice any of the Skills that helped him get his life back. Even worse, he had a scary rash all over his body. The doctors had told him it was a stress-related reaction of the body and that he needed to change the way he lived immediately to prevent serious damage. Not only was he super miserable, but now his health and life were in danger.

When he told me the whole story about how this year went, I asked him, "What do you think you must do to recover and get your amazing life back?"

"I must get back to using The Method," he replied.

I knew that this was the right answer, but I wanted him to

decide it for himself. And he did. Next day, he went back to using The Method again.

A month later, his life was once again skyrocketing toward the direction of his own desires.

IF YOU ARE NOT WINNING, YOU ARE LOSING

There's a saying which goes like this: "Everybody wants to go to heaven, but nobody wants to die."

Everybody wants to be healthy and energetic, have amazing relationships, live the most inspiring and successful Mission, be in the best emotional state, achieve financial abundance, and experience all the best things life has to offer. But nobody is willing to do what it takes. And even if you think you're doing it … well, I know you're not. That was my case and the case of everyone around me before we started using this system.

We want stuff, but then we don't do anything about it. We say we do something, but we merely scratch the surface of it. And even if we go deeper into one area, we forget all the rest, which simply doesn't work (remember the wheel).

You see, the world has become physically and mentally obese. We fill our bodies with junk, the same way we fill our everyday lives with bullshit decisions that are far from what is in our best interest. And we find all the best excuses to make ourselves believe that this stupid behavior is perfectly normal.

If you can't make the best conscious decision about what you must eat, how the hell do you think you're going to make the best decision about what's best for your future, your finances, your Mission, your children, the world around you? You won't! You just won't!

If you want to continue that way, fine. That's your choice. But you might as well say goodbye to most of the amazing things you want to experience in life. And if you think that such behavior is the easier path in life, look five, ten, twenty years in the future and try to imagine how things might look and how it might feel if you don't change now…

On the other side, there is a different world. A world where you are authentic, and you see and name things for what they are. You take responsibility and make a plan to experience life the way you want to. To get the things you want to get. You put this system to work, and you show yourself and others what self-discipline can do in just a few months.

And you build the health. You get the relationships. You start living this inspiring Mission and achieve more than ever before. You experience life with a set of new positive emotions. You create and secure your financial abundance. And you manufacture the lifestyle of your dreams. And you do it all together. Without compromise.

We need a bulletproof Method. A Method that will help us become and stay disciplined. A Method that will help us create a personalized ecosystem that is filled with the best we can create. With conscious, strategic, great choices. Not with junk. We need a Method that strategizes our lives for success, health, and excitement.

No real high-performer ever wakes up and lives his/her day without a very clear plan what he/she needs to do next. Not only do they know what they're going to, why they're going to do it, and when they're going to do it, but they actually go and do it. But you know what? Most high-performers in different areas (sports, business, health) are not high-performers in life. Not because they can't be, but because they don't take a holistic approach. And that's exactly what we are doing here. Becoming high-performers in life.

We need to follow this simple approach. I call it "THE 4Ws," and it looks like this:

(1) What I need to do

(2) Why I need to do it

(3) When I need to do it

(4) Well, do it!

Do you know who is best at designing and executing such a holistic approach in life? It's nature.

You see, nature is designed to function the way it does to create and sustain life. For some unknown reason, it knows what it needs to do, why it needs to do it, when it needs to do it, and most importantly — it never fails to deliver. If it did fail to deliver even at one of its critical tasks (let's say the Earth forgot to rotate yesterday), we wouldn't be having this conversation now. We wouldn't exist.

Nothing in nature happens by chance. Everything is connected and serves a specific purpose. But we still think we can keep on living without a system and without methodical decisions and actions. And we expect the universe to come and deliver all the stuff we want as breakfast-in-bed hotel service. We'll have to wait a long time for that meal.

Each decision, each action, every single day, is connected to the results we are going to get. **Just as spring brings life to flowers and the moon moves tides on the shores, nothing is simply chance. Everything happens for a reason. Everything is a routine.**

That's the tool I realized I needed to create for myself. I knew I had to have a great strategy and become perfectly self-disciplined to be able to experience the lifestyle of my dreams. And I did it. It's time you do it too.

This part of the book was the missing link in my chain. I've learned a ton from sports, business, and personal development, but I needed what you are about to learn here to be able to start living the lifestyle I wanted. Without this piece, none of what I shared with you so far would really matter.

It's this piece that brings the whole system together. It's this piece that helps you implement all the best techniques in your life. It's this piece that keeps your life wheel growing and strong. It's this piece that helps you always stay on track. It's this piece that helps you deliver in everything that matters — just like nature does.

It is because of the lack of this piece that people learn from seminars, courses, books, then they apply the knowledge for a week or two, and in a month they are back where they started. We are never going to have any more of that!

We already spoke about how we can master a single hour of our time with Success Blocks. Now, let's see how we can master our days and weeks so that we can regain our power and join the 0.1% Club.

17

THE PERFECT WEEK

Contrary to some clichéd expressions, you don't win the day by winning the morning. The same way you don't win a race by winning the start. You win the day by winning the damn day. Same goes for a race and everything else. Morning rituals can only do that much if you don't have day rituals.

But winning the day is not enough either. We need to look at the bigger picture. Why? Because we don't practice all our Skills on a daily basis. We need a week for that. So we will focus on creating the perfect week. Winning the week is extremely powerful. And you only need to do it fifty-two times per year.

Here's an example for comparison, from how my weeks used to go to how they go now.

BEFORE

I would wake up between seven and ten; it really depended on how tired I was. Some might think I was lucky being a CEO, but honestly, it wasn't doing any good for me, for the team, or for our company's goals. I would rush to the shower because I had "no time to lose" (I'd usually wake up thirty minutes before a meeting or before going to the office). I'd think about all the crap that might come up throughout the day under the shower. By the time I got dressed and was ready to go out, my hands were already shaking from stress.

On the way to work, I'd check social media, news, and best of all, my email. Guess what? There was always something "very important" in the inbox that I needed to take care of first thing in the office.

I'd keep an open-door policy at the office where any of the twenty-five team members could walk in at any time and kill my attempts at being productive (not their fault, but mine).

At lunch, I'd order KFC or some other fast food option because "I'm busy" (better put — lazy and dumb).

Then I'd continue without being able to achieve much of what was really important until everyone else left the office (about 7:00 p.m.)

Time for work! I'd sit down and do my best to focus with an empty mental battery until 3-4:00 a.m. I'd eat something fast and maybe drink a bit of water at some point when I remembered.

I'd drive back home and go to sleep.

Day over! Game over!

Next day — repeat!

If you're interested in Saturday and Sunday, I'd use them to try to catch up on all the things I couldn't do throughout the week. I'd maybe squeeze an hour to visit my parents and eat some real food.

Does some of that sound familiar to you? Do you also "lack the time" to work out, meditate, read, spend time with your friends and family, work on new skill development, grow your business?

I hear you! That was me, 100 percent. It was. Until I decided that it wouldn't be.

NOW

I wake up at 6:00 a.m. after a nearly eight-hour sleep (Skill #1: The Sweet Dreams). I drink some water and jump straight on my trampoline. I do one minute of jumping and intense breathing. I then do my visualization practice (Skill #2: The Brave Visualization).

Five out of seven days, I continue with a forty-minute workout (Skill #3: The Power Moves).

At 7:00 a.m. it's time for my morning meditation (Skill #4: The Present Moment), which I usually do on the rooftop of our building.

A healthy breakfast (Skill #5: The Sacred Breakfast), my daily supplements, and a cold shower make the end of my morning routine. Yep, you heard me right. Cold shower. It's the best way to kill inflammation, wake up the body, and start the day with something hard and painful; your daily struggles seem much less intimidating after a thirty-second freezing shower. That's one of the Level 2 Skills I'm going to share with you in a bit.

By 8:30 a.m., I'm ready to start my first sixty-minute Success Block, followed by a five-minute Recharge session (Skill #6: The Success Blocks). All the water I'll drink for the day is on my desk (Skill #8: The Pure Water). I do my best to schedule all meetings and calls on Monday morning. Why Monday morning? Because then I can get results before the end of the week. By batching them all in one big block, I also make sure I save energy by staying in one mode for longer — calls and meetings, instead of constantly switching between talking to other people and focusing on my own tasks. All meetings, calls, and Success Blocks are scheduled in my calendar on Saturday (Skill #13: The Game Plan).

I repeat the cycle until lunch at 12:30 p.m., and then I move on again to complete a total of nine super-productive work hours. It may not sound like too much, and that's the best part. It isn't. But it's incredible how much more you can create in nine perfectly focused hours, compared with twelve or even fourteen hours of scattered-focus work. Especially when you do your breathing and recharging exercises between each one. You can work between 8:30 a.m. to 6:30 p.m. (with a one-hour lunch break) and achieve much more than 99.9 percent of the world. Why? Because everybody else works the way I used to. And it's a waste.

After I'm done with my Success Blocks for the day, I have thirty minutes for email, social media, and sometimes a quick check on the news headlines. I don't allow myself to do any of that before my work day is over (Skill #7: The Limitless Action). None of these actions requires my best quality focus. I certainly don't want to waste it early in the morning.

At 7:00 p.m. I do my afternoon mediation (that's a Level 2 Skill too) to transition from being fired up to a more grounded, relaxed state of mind. This helps me separate work from everything else and cleanse any potential negative emotions before I dive into family, friends, and hobbies time.

At 7:30 p.m. we have a great healthy dinner, usually followed by a short walk. I'll talk to my family and one of my friends (Skill #9: The Inner Circle). Then it's playtime. My wife and I will watch some documentaries, talk about books, and discuss business ideas.

Before I shut off all screens at 10:00 p.m., I make a few screenshots and share the results from The Method with my friends (Skill #15: The Secret Mastermind) and now with you on Instagram. I will then read a book (Skill #11: The Personal University) and take some notes before we go to bed at 10:30 p.m.

On Saturdays, I wake up later — at 7:30 a.m. I follow my mourning routine and do two Success Blocks. I plan the week ahead, and after that, it's all about family and friends until Monday morning. I'd also think of a cool little something to surprise my wife somewhere in the week (Skill #12: The Weekly Surprise).

If at this point I see that I still haven't done anything great for another person (Skill #10: The Joyful Tears), I might think of someone I've never met who has influenced my life positively. I'll find them on Instagram or Facebook and will write them a "thank-you" message explaining how exactly they've influenced my journey. Or I might call a friend to thank him/her for something they did. If I'm outside, I'll just step out of my way to make someone feel amazing.

In the meantime, my automated money machine will be working for me while I sleep (Skill #14: The Financial Freedom). No need to do anything here other than take a peek every now and then and feel great for being responsible and taking the time to set it up.

My usual day looks something like that (see 0.1% Mode on the right in the provided image). Take note of the subtle differences with 99% Mode (left) and 1% Mode (middle) ? I've lived for a long time in the first two states. But once I tested 0.1% Mode for the first time, I realized that these small changes made for a massive transformation in my life experience and the results I'm able to achieve. I know that once you give it a try, you'll never want to go back.

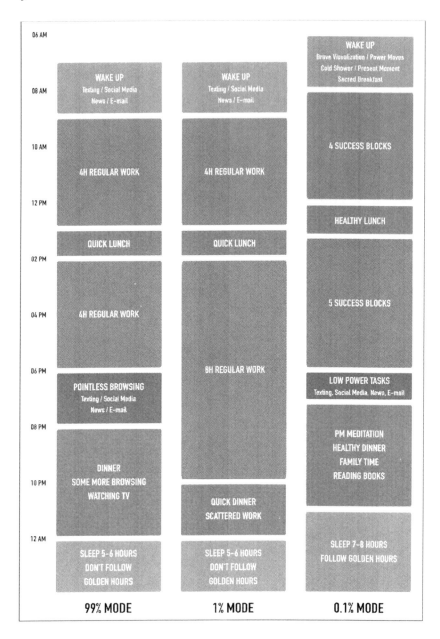

Don't worry if your lifestyle differs somewhat or completely from mine, my friend. That won't prevent you from taking advantage of much of what the system has to offer. Just stick with me.

So far, so good. But how the hell do you become so disciplined when life is just so complicated and messy? That's where The Method comes into play!

What you are about to learn is the simplest thing you've ever heard that has the power to give you everything you've ever wanted.

Let me introduce you to...

18

THE UNFAIR ADVANTAGE (A.K.A. THE METHOD)

S ome people just make life and success look easy. And that used to piss me off! Not because I envied them, but because I was so eager to learn how to make it happen in my life as well.

I had a meeting with the CEO of one of the biggest companies in Eastern Europe. I was five minutes early when I entered the building, so I had a little time to look around. The place looked like a huge spaceship. What was most impressive was how clean and shiny everything was. It was just perfect.

I went to the second floor and found my way to the meeting room. The CEO's secretary welcomed me to his office and said he would be there any moment.

Right in front of me, there was a huge, luxurious desk with a computer screen on top. On the left side of the room, there was a large oval table next to a glass wall with a beautiful view. Just like at the entrance of the building, everything in this office was perfectly set up and clean. Everything had its designated place.

What really impressed me was that there was nothing on the CEO's desk (I immediately compared it with my desk in my office). There wasn't a pen, a piece of paper, not even a single freakin' sticky note on the computer screen.

Seconds before the scheduled time of our meeting, the CEO entered with a huge smile. We exchanged warm welcome hugs and started talking. The guy was strikingly smart. Super sharp. But at the same time, he didn't make me feel stupid or any less than himself (even though I sure was back then). In fact, talking to him made me feel more inspired and enthusiastic. His incredible energy lifted me up for my personal business ideas and life — stuff that had nothing to do with our planned conversation.

But I couldn't stop thinking about what I wanted to ask him…

"Hey, before we continue, can you tell me something? How do you make all this possible? You run this huge, complex organization. How can you take the time to meet me? You came perfectly on time, you are not stressed or rushing for anything, you are in great shape … and how the hell do you manage to have your desk perfectly clean without even a single piece of paper? Do you even work in this office?"

He laughed and went on to tell me about the way he organizes his life. Not just his work life but also his personal time with family and friends. This conversation continued for hours, first in the office and then in a great restaurant over dinner.

At first, I couldn't believe it was possible to live such a kickass life. But there it was. This man somehow found a way to do it. And now he was leading a company with over three thousand employees and total assets of nearly a billion dollars. More importantly, though, he was one of the happiest people I've ever met.

The way I saw it, he had an Unfair Advantage. And I wasn't

going to experience my life in any lesser way than that. I wanted this Unfair Advantage. And I know you want it too. Don't you?

Well, here it is.

The only thing you need to do to get the Unfair Advantage is measure your Skills performance.

What do I mean by that?

Do you know someone who needed to lose weight and went on to achieve that goal? Have you seen how they progress and achieve great results when they start journaling what and how much they eat? Why is that? The reason is very simple. If we don't monitor and measure our performance, we usually act like idiots.

I used to think that we are all very smart. I believed that we remember all the important things we must do.

Do you remember how many times you went to the gym last week? Or how many times you ate something you said you wouldn't? What about your focused work blocks? How many of those did you complete last Wednesday? How much water did you drink? Did you make time for your family and friends every day? Did you talk to your grandparents last week? Did you meditate every day? How about going to bed and waking up on time? Did you practice your new habits and skills? Did you take your supplements four days ago?

I know. You have absolutely no idea. Neither did I. Here's the irony. We all know that these are the most important things we must do to live incredible lives, but we just don't do them.

And as simple as all that may sound, measuring our Skills performance is what makes the whole difference in the end. This is what gives us the Unfair Advantage and makes us look like rock stars next to everyone else in the world who doesn't do that. Just like I looked next to that CEO who had figured out how to play the game long before I did. In the end, this Unfair Advantage helps us shape our lives the way we want to. And without it, we are back to acting like chimps and ruining our lives, just like my friend Bryan did. No offense, Bryan. You know I've done it too.

GIVE ME THE UNFAIR ADVANTAGE!

This whole book was slowly leading to this part. That's the most basic and at the same time most important thing you are going to learn here. It's a little game we are going to start playing. It's the game of our lives. Only this time, we are going to win.

You already know the Big Fifteen Skills:

Skill #1: THE SWEET DREAMS
Skill #2: THE BRAVE VISUALIZATION
Skill #3: THE POWER MOVES
Skill #4: THE PRESENT MOMENT
Skill #5: THE SACRED BREAKFAST
Skill #6: THE SUCCESS BLOCKS
Skill #7: THE LIMITLESS ACTION
Skill #8: THE PURE WATER
Skill #9: THE INNER CIRCLE
Skill #10: THE JOYFUL TEARS
Skill #11: THE PERSONAL UNIVERSITY
Skill #12: THE WEEKLY SURPRISE
Skill #13: THE GAME PLAN
Skill #14: THE FINANCIAL FREEDOM
Skill #15: THE SECRET MASTERMIND

If you need to refresh your memory or notes about how to practice any of them, you can always go back to the previous STEP.

Here's what we are going to do now. Get ready to experience the best week of your life!

I want you to get a piece of paper and two pens (red and green). If that's too old-school for you (which I hope it is), I want you to go online to www.simeonivanov.com/products/book-course and download the Excel sheet that I've created for you in section "The Method." If Excel is too old-school for you (which I again hope it is) and you have a smartphone, I want you to download a phone app called "Way of Life!" (the developer of the app is Way of Life ApS). Whichever of the three you are most comfortable with, I want you to do it now before we continue. Keep in mind that the smartphone solution is far superior to any of the other solutions, but that doesn't mean The Method cannot work without a mobile app.

As I'm writing this, the phone app is free to start with, but it might cost a few dollars when you read this. If it's something like four or five dollars, buy it. It will be the best money you've ever spent. I'm not associated in any way with the creators of the app, and I'm not paid to say that. It's just the best possible tool you can use to get the results we are seeking. This app is the tool that everyone around me has been using for years to run their own systems. If you don't have the money to afford it right now, I understand. That's why I've created the free Excel sheet for you. Go and download the app or the file now before we continue.

Are you ready? Let's move on!

Whichever tool you picked, I want you to include all fifteen Skills in the same order (I've done that for you in the Excel sheet).

If you are going to use paper (please don't), your page must look like that:

```
MON  TUE  WED  THU  FRI  SAT  SUN
THE SWEET DREAMS

THE BRAVE VISUALIZATION

THE POWER MOVES

THE PRESENT MOMENT

THE SACRED BREAKFAST

THE SUCCESS BLOCKS

THE LIMITLESS ACTION

THE PURE WATER

        and  so  on . . .
```

If you bought the app, you chose the best option of all. Open it up and click on the + sign to include your Skills one by one; the app calls them "Journals." Don't pay attention to that difference. We are going to call them Skills anyway. In the end, the home screen of the app must look like that (add whatever emojis you like to make it more engaging and motivating).

All you need to do from now on, starting tomorrow morning, is remind yourself of what every Skill means, how you are going to practice it, and then hit the START button first thing in the morning.

Here's how you will be using The Method. Once you are all set and your Skills are all in place, it's time to follow these few simple steps:

STEP 1: SET UP THE REMINDERS

Set three alarms (that repeat every day) on your phone as follows:

ALARM #1: Set it to ring two minutes after your wake-up time (chosen from your golden hours testing) and name it "0.1%"
ALARM #2: Set it for 12:00 p.m. and name it "0.1%"
ALARM #3: Set it for 8:00 p.m. and name it "0.1%"

These are your three reminders to open the app (or the Excel/paper journal) and fill your results. You need these reminders because this is something completely new for you, and you will keep forgetting it at first (trust me on that).

You can also set up some reminders through the app settings, but I've found that alarms work better because they are significantly more disturbing. And you want to be disturbed for this.

STEP 2: TURN ON THE BADGE

If you are going to use the app, turn the "Badge" ON. By doing that, you will be able to see a little red bubble over the app icon that will tell you how many incomplete Skills you have left for the day without needing to open the app.

STEP 3: HOW TO MARK THE SKILLS

Whenever you successfully complete a Skill for the day, you go to the app (or Excel/journal) and mark it in GREEN. The first thing you do when you wake up is to go to the app and mark whether you have successfully followed your golden hours (The Sweet Dreams). If you did, you put GREEN. If you didn't for any reason (you went to bed or woke up later), you put RED.

If a Skill is not to be performed every single day:

The Power Moves (I aim for five times a week)
The Success Blocks (I don't do any on Sunday)
The Joyful Tears (I aim for a minimum of once a week)
The Weekly Surprise (I aim for a minimum of once a week)
The Game Plan (I do it only on Saturdays)

then you put a SKIP for the days where you are either resting or it's simply not the day for that Skill (see image). If you are using the Excel sheet or your journal, simply put the gray color or make a few black lines like that [//////] to know that it is a SKIP.

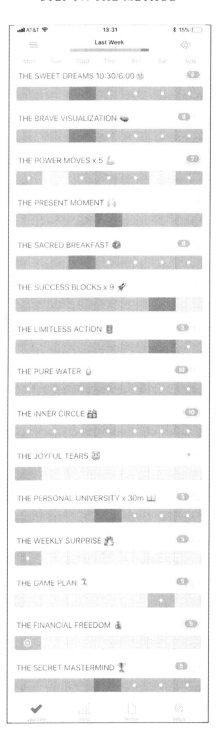

Note how you can add sleep times, as well as, "x 3" or "x 5" to make it even clearer for yourself and your Mastermind group members what you consider a successful completion of the Skill. For me, The Power Moves are a success if I manage to complete five workouts a week. Hence, the "x 5" you see in the image example above.

STEP 4: LEARN AND GROW

At the end of each week, go to the "Trend" menu to see your progress. That's where the app really excels compared to the other options. See how many REDS and how many GREENS you have. Look at your overall score and share it with your Mastermind group. After a couple of weeks, you will start seeing your progress in comparison to the previous weeks, and that will serve as extra motivation. Use the numerical setting and the bar chart for six or twelve weeks. See image example.

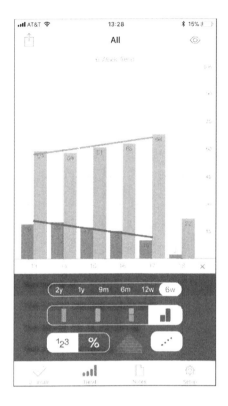

STEP 5: NEVER, EVER BULLSHIT YOURSELF

Be true to yourself. If you've missed a Skill for any reason — it's RED. There's nothing worse than lying to yourself.

STEP 6: MAKE IT FUN

Don't forget to make it fun to keep yourself in the game. Get a few friends to set it up as well and start sharing your Skills with each other at the end of the day (this is your Secret Mastermind Skill). To share your progress, simply make a few screenshots and send those through whatever messaging app you use. Remember, don't use this space for sharing photos of your dog or screenshots from 9GAG.

Help each other to do better and improve your Skills performance with time.

Once again, if you don't initially find anyone to practice this Skill with, you can make screenshots and post your Skill performance on Instagram or Facebook and tag @0.1book or @simeonivanov. I'll post my own performance in these pages every day as a "Story," and I'll do my best to check yours out and see if you need any guidance.

STEP 7: DON'T THINK

Don't take key Skills out because you think they are already a habit. They are not. I removed The Present Moment a few years ago, only to realize I'd stopped meditating a few months later. Everybody else who I've coached has gone through this same mistake, and sometimes it takes ages to realize you've been tricked by your own mind. We have so many things going on in our lives. We forget. Don't trust your memory. You don't need to remember anything, and you don't need to think. Use The Method instead. It will never forget.

So here's what you are going to do tomorrow. You'll wake up at your planned time, you'll open the app, and mark GREEN or RED, depending on whether you've accomplished your Sweet Dreams Skill. Then, on to Brave Visualization. After that, Power Moves and so on, until you finish the day, mark all your Skills in the appropriate color, and send the screenshots to your Mastermind members.

The Method will be your daily guide. If for a second you wonder what your next best move is, simply open the app and check out what you next Skill is. Then go on and complete it or skip it if it's not the day for it.

Note that if this sequence doesn't work for your lifestyle (e.g., you can only do The Power Moves in the afternoon), you can rearrange the Skills the way they work best for you. But no matter what, do not delete any Skill unless there is a medical or other very serious reason why you should never follow such a habit.

19

WHY THE METHOD WORKS

During my time in the medical field, our company was selling the most advanced medical equipment in the world. Our team got trained and executed major projects for the complete remodeling of surgical departments. And we implemented some pretty crazy stuff in those operating rooms.

One innovation that was a major breakthrough all around the world was an Integrated Operating Room with Neurosurgical Navigation. What this "integration" means is that most pieces of equipment in the room can "communicate" with each other: table, lights, computers, screens, cameras, even surgical tools.

When in action, the room "knows" which patient is coming in, what condition he/she has, what part of the body needs to be operated on, and what kind of equipment and tools are required for a successful surgery. An automatic checklist is generated for the physician's team, which only needs to show (literally) to the system's camera that they have all the required tools. The computers won't start operating before this step is successfully completed.

"So what?" someone could say. "Big deal." Right?

Well, let's see. Try to imagine the following.

A surgery in a regular (nonintegrated) operating room starts. The team hasn't implemented any checklist procedures. They work hard for an hour, open the patient's body, get to the problematic area ... and realize they are missing the tool needed to make the final step of the operation. They anxiously start running around, blaming whoever was responsible for having the tool there. They call other departments, trying to borrow one of their tools. During this time, the patient gets extra sedation (very bad for the patient) to make sure he is kept unconscious. Anyway, with an hour delay (very bad for the team and the hospital), they are done, and they do the last stitch. Mission successful ... ooor maybe not! They realize they've operated on the wrong leg. Oops!

You don't want to be the one sharing this lovely news with the family of the patient.

This is not a fictitious story. Things like that happen in hospitals. Why? Physicians are pros, right? Yes, they are. But they are human too. And humans make mistakes.

This is why high-responsibility organizations (some of them) like airlines, hospitals, and others are creating checklists for their operations. You must never trust anyone to remember. You must never trust yourself on that either.

But you can trust The Method.

The Method works for a few reasons. First — it's simple. There's no useless functionality. Second — it's visual. Visual and color-coded motivates more than plain words. When you see you have three REDs on sleeping, and you know sleep is important for your success, health, and happiness, your brain triggers a response. That response is crucial. Third — it consists of everything that makes your life great. These are not just some random Skills. It's your life. Fourth — it visualizes your growth or degradation. What you will notice is that the Trends (improving or getting worse) are closely connected to how you will feel about yourself, your health, your energy, your Mission. When you follow the Skills, and you achieve great results (more GREEN), you will feel great, and your measurable, real-life results will be there to prove it too. When you don't, well, you'll see for yourself and will let me know what you think about the difference. Last, but not least, using The Method will help you spot patterns and causations. For example, you didn't hit your sleeping goal two days in a row — your work performance went down. You didn't hydrate enough for three days — you started getting headaches. You had no idea where all of that came from before, because you didn't have even the simplest piece of data to evaluate the situation. But now you do, and you can easily find the reasons behind your lack of performance or even some of your illnesses. Most importantly, you can use this information to quickly and efficiently eliminate the cause of the symptoms. How powerful an advantage is that?

Becoming a master of action (and the right action, especially) is effortless when you follow The Method, and you practice your routine long enough. If you don't set it up and use it diligently, the unimportant distractions will find a way to creep in and steal your time and your life.

When we repeatedly do something every day or every week at the appropriate scheduled time, research has proven that our brains create previously nonexistent neuron connections. Our brain develops to accommodate our new actions as a routine. Hence, if you had previously found it difficult to get to the gym or concentrate and execute at work, following The Method will only make each of those things easier and more enjoyable.

That's the moment when it will start looking to others as if you have developed an Unfair Advantage and things are just happening for you. But the truth is that you took the time to set this system up, and you took the first steps that will now be making all the difference you have been searching for.

Just as your phone or an Apple Watch reminds you to make more steps throughout the day, and it shows you if you haven't been taking great care of your physical activity, The Method gives you the visual representation of how well you perform in every important area of life.

If the most successful companies spend millions of dollars to generate and visualize important data that helps them make better decisions (sales, costs, customer satisfaction, etc.), we must do the same for our lives.

When you personally set up your Skills with a level of integrity and higher aspirations, when you start sharing your results with others, the level of both conscious and unconscious commitment skyrockets compared with if you just think you should do something.

Thinking you should doesn't work. We all know that.

I've worked for so long with The Method that it has become a barometer for the quality of my life. If I get a full GREEN day, I feel amazing, and my results show it. If for some reason, I get too many REDs on my Skills, I don't feel so good, and my results suffer. Why? Because I haven't done the things that help get me closer to where I want to be.

The Method, I'm sure, is not perfect. It'll get better and better with your feedback and your help. I'll give you all updates in your   free   online   course   at www.simeonivanov.com/products/book-course so you won't need to buy an updated version of the book when there is one (that wouldn't be fair). Whenever we (you, other readers, and I) learn something new and better, you'll be notified and will be able to implement it straight away.

Since I started teaching people how to implement The Method

in their lives, I've heard a lot of objections. I know you might have some too, so I'd like to share those with you here.

O&A (OBJECTIONS AND ANSWERS)

"Simeon, that's too simple, man. How is that going to change anything?"

Thank you for noticing, Sherlock! I know it's simple. Follow it strictly for a week, and then we'll talk.

"I don't have time for that."

Bullshit. You don't have time because you don't use The Method. You lose so much more time when you feel like crap, and you run around being unproductive. I'll prove to you that you have time for everything. Just start. Give it a week.

"It's too much work."

No, it isn't. It takes ten minutes to set it up. Your thumbs won't hurt from clicking on the phone screen. I've done it. It's safe. What's too much work and what takes too much time is wandering around without a clear purpose and plan.

"It's too complicated."

Is it? It's like your schedule at school. You know exactly what you need to do and when you need to do it. Only it's the really important things in your life and not something you give zero shits about. That's it. I've given you a step-by-step guide on how to set it up. If you have a question, send it as a comment in the online course, but don't make excuses why you won't give this a try.

"It's not fun enough. You know, I'm more of an artistic person. I'm not in the military."

So you are creative, right? Be creative when it comes to figuring out how to make your life work. Don't use your amazing creativity as an excuse not to take control. An artist with a clear purpose and action plan is a successful and fulfilled artist.

Some people think that this way of living is too strict and it eliminates freedom. I used to suspect so too. And I was wrong. Living like this creates freedom that you have never experienced before. Structured, planned freedom you can actually enjoy because you've done the work that matters. Because you've taken amazing care of everything important. That's what I call living!

"I don't remember to do it..."

Put some alarms and reminders. Put some notes in places you'll see them. Make it hard not to do it and easy to do it. Is your life important enough?

"I didn't do it for a week, something came up, and then I stopped."

Who cares!? Start again! It doesn't matter that you've stopped for a while if that's in the past. It's gone. Start over. Focus on now and figure out how not to stop the next time. Remember what happened with my friend Bryan. You don't want to repeat his mistake.

20

LEVEL 2 SKILLS

I f you are already a pro in any of the Big Fifteen Skills, that's great. What you can do is use a Level 2 Skill instead or add an extra Skill to your set.

Here are a few examples:

EXAMPLE 1: YOU ARE ALREADY EATING HEALTHY, AND YOU ARE LOOKING FOR THE EXTRA EDGE

Obviously, if you are already eating super healthy but you are looking for the next level, The Sacred Breakfast won't be enough for you. In this case, I've personally added a Level 2 Skill to my Method. Here it is:

SKILL: THE PERFECT DIET

For me, this Skill represents the following: no red meat, no gluten, no eggs, no dairy, no sugar, no alcohol.

Do I follow this every single day? No. Why? Because I love pizza and I love red meat. So I allow myself to have two cheat meals (note that I say meals, not days) during every week. One of those meals is a juicy beef steak. The other is a tasty pizza with a can of Coke. During those two days, I'll "SKIP" instead of marking it "RED." But if I eat more than two of those meals during the week, I'll mark the third one in "RED" to know that I've broken my own rules.

You can include any food you perceive as unhealthy in this Skill. You can also include certain drinks (coffee, Coke, packaged juices), or even smoking.

EXAMPLE 2: YOU ARE ALREADY FIT, AND THE POWER MOVES ARE TOO LITTLE

Great job! All you need to do is to set a higher limit for the same Skill. Instead of "never skip two days in a row," it can be "work out five times a week" or whatever works for you. Either way, no need to change the Skill. Simply add a rule to it and start following it. You can name your Skill in The Method as follows: "THE POWER MOVES x 5."

EXAMPLE 3: YOU WANT TO BE EVEN COOLER

If you want to know what's cooler than being cool, it's time to start your ice baths or cold showers. Put "Hey Ya!" by OutKast on the speaker and let the fun begin!

I love that one. I already told you about it. I personally do:

SKILL: THE COLD SHOWER every morning. I go for the shower instead of the bath because the bath takes too much time to prepare, which ads extra complexity to my day. But the shower is easy. When I'm done washing, I just turn the knob to maximum cold for thirty seconds and enjoy the party (I don't wash my head with the cold water). After thirty seconds, I turn back to warm water to finish on a more comfortable note.

While under the cold water I have a little add-on ritual which is: I tell myself out loud that "I am enough" and then move on with mentally forgiving someone (often myself) about something.

Note: don't try the cold shower if you have any medical condition (especially but not limited to heart disease). Consult with your doctor and read about it first.

EXAMPLE 4: THE POTENTIAL IS LIMITLESS

Once you are a Method Superstar, you can add whatever other crazy Skill that you want to experiment with or you already know adds great value to your days. People who are using The Method have been really creative with inventing new ways to boost their performance in different areas of life.

An important note here: never include more than twenty Skills in your Method. I've been testing this thing for three years now, and I've seen how people mess up their game when they try to put too much on their plates. Try to keep it as simple and as actionable as possible. Try to stay focused on the big picture.

If you step on the wrong foot and mess it up, you can always go back to the Big Fifteen Skills and start over from there. You'll begin to realize that at the end of the day that's all we really need to be able to get everything we want from life.

You are now ready to hit the START button. Have you set up your Skills and the alarms in your phone? Promise yourself that you will begin your day by opening the app and hitting the GREEN or RED on your first Skill! Promise yourself that you will continue marking your progress until the end of the week! That's all you need: a single week. Once you go past that threshold, you will never want to leave your Unfair Advantage behind again.

Make a promise now! Tomorrow, you will begin your new life.

You've come a long way, my friend. I'm so excited for you! I know exactly what The Method will do for you if you follow it strictly. I can't wait for you to share your success story with me!

But we have one last STEP without which the system is incomplete.

Let's learn why we must always do...

STEP V: THE RESTART

THE POWER OF REFLECTION

"No artist is pleased. There is no satisfaction whatever at any time. There is only a queer, divine dissatisfaction; a blessed unrest that keeps us marching and makes us more alive than the others."

— MARTHA GRAHAM

The game of life is a never-ending process. You can't stop playing and expect to stay in the same place because everything else around you is moving forward. The bus is waiting for no one.

Thus, we must keep on marching. We must be aware whenever a new wall is forming that is preventing us from reaching the next level. We must constantly reshape and enhance our Character to correspond with the ever-expanding Mission in our lives. And we must always stick to our Method to improve our performance in the game and to make sure we are always on the right track.

The game of life is nothing more than a constant journey of growth. And it's in that journey that we get to experience who we really are. It's in that journey that we get to find success and happiness.

21

ACHIEVEMENT IS TEMPORARY

"W as that it?" That's one of the most common questions I used to ask myself every time I achieved something I previously considered to be "great." The emotional high has always been much shorter than I've expected. Why? Because of human nature. The moment we achieve something, we simply raise the bar and switch our focus to the next level. And that can be a great thing and a terrible thing. It's all up to how you decide to use it.

It's great if you learn to enjoy the game you are playing for the game itself. Achievement is temporary. The game of life lasts forever. It's tough if you play someone else's game. And if you are miserable throughout the journey, no achievement will ever make you happy.

But the game is not the achievement. The game is the game. It's the days, the weeks, the months, and the years. It's your life, every single moment. Chasing useless achievements that won't bring you anything of real value is simply a waste of time. It's a waste of energy. A waste of brainpower. A waste of life. A waste of you. Don't fall into this trap.

You want to play a game that inspires you to grow. A game that matters. A challenging game. You want to follow goals that are nearly impossible to achieve. You want to be yourself, fully expressed. There's only one you on this planet. You might as well show yourself and the world what you are capable of.

The achievements are simply milestones along the way, but they are not your source of happiness — you are. The game you purposefully design and play is.

If we are to enjoy life, we need to learn to live for the game. For the journey itself. Not just for the achievements.

WHY KEEP GROWING?

A couple of years ago I asked one of my childhood friends what he was up to lately. He shared that he was watching a new TV show. I asked him whether he was learning something valuable or whether it was a comedy. His answer was priceless. "It's a great show when I want to kill some time," he said.

I don't want to preach, but if you know people who are also looking for ways to kill some time, ask them to put their shit together and start living again.

Nobody wants to kill time. We all want more time. That's just the worst excuse ever not to take responsibility for all the misery in our lives. We all want to live exciting lives. And we all know that there are certain things we need to do to achieve that.

So why do we want to never stop growing? There are a few great reasons.

First, you'll never be bored again. I haven't really been bored since I was a kid, so boredom is a concept I have a hard time understanding. But a big part for me of not getting bored has been my drive to excel in certain areas of my life. Hence, my lack of need to kill any time whatsoever by watching useless TV shows. Don't get me wrong; I love TV shows, but I never use them to kill time. I use them to learn or be entertained. I schedule these things in my calendar while doing my Game Plan (Skill #13).

Second, that's the only way to get what you want in life. And a huge part of what you want is to grow in those key areas that make your life wheel. You know they'll bring you more meaning, more joy, more happiness. After a certain level, growing your income and your possessions won't make you any happier. We all know that. Don't let money become your drug that you chase just for the sake of getting some more. What will make you happier is growing as a person. Serving more people through your Mission. Growing in your relationships. Becoming emotionally bulletproof. Creating the energy and time that will allow you to make an impact and enjoy life the way you want to.

Some people say that asking for more is a recipe for unhappiness. I say asking for nothing is a recipe for premature death. You die a thousand times before you physically die. Tell me the name of one person you admire who asked for nothing in his life. Even the most spiritual beings in this world have their Missions to get to a deeper state of meditation, to better themselves and the world around them. Even gods have their wants.

We are born to struggle, to evolve, and grow. If we weren't, we'd still be living in caves and communicating like monkeys. So consider the lack of desire for growth completely unnatural and massively damaging. You might want to share this chapter with some of your friends.

22

HOW AND WHEN TO RESTART

After you've fully implemented your system and you've lived it for six months, it's time for a Restart. Think of that as a necessary self-reflecting session required for reaching the next level of growth. Why six months?

Some people review their lives every twelve months. And most people ... most people do it the week before they die. That's a little too late for major changes.

We want to do it more often for several important reasons. First, the world is changing faster than ever before. Second, the more often we reflect, the faster we'll grow. We'll also learn sooner if we've been going in a direction that doesn't serve our predesigned lifestyle and purpose. We don't want to wait twelve months to see that the course has changed. Third, when you use this system, you'll be a different person in six months. With all the new experiences, with all the new achievements and knowledge, you'll inevitably build new subconscious Walls (STEP I of the book), but also new Values, new Aspirations, new Goals (STEP II of the book). You might even find new Skills that work even better

(STEP III of the book), and you'll want to implement them in your Method (STEP IV of the book).

The only thing we need to do to Restart the system is to go through several of the exercises, just like we did in the past days. When you go through them again, it will take much less time, since you are already familiar with the concepts and you don't need to reread the whole book.

Here's the easiest and fastest way to do your Restart (instead of going through the whole book again):

Schedule an event in your calendar for the date exactly six months from now. Set it so you'll receive an email when the time comes (I use Google Calendar for that). Call the event "0.1% SYSTEM RESTART" or something that will remind you of what you want to do.

Include this link: www.simeonivanov.com/products/book-course to the event. When the time comes, click the link, and it will take you to the free online course, where I'll guide you step by step through the process of restarting and going through all the exercises (visit section "The Restart"). You'll also be able to find all useful updates there and share your thoughts and your success story with me and other readers and active users of the system.

My friend, I want to tell you one last thing...

IT'S TIME

"If you think you are too small to make a difference, try sleeping with a mosquito."

— THE DALAI LAMA

One day, you and I will most certainly find a better solution and a better system to help us create the things we want in our lives. Sooner or later, that's what happens with every piece of advice and with everything we know about how the world works. We learn how to do things better.

If (when) that happens, I suggest you rip the useless pages off that book and wipe your back parts with them. I'll still be your friend, I promise. That's certainly what I'll do. But until then, give everything you've learned a chance. Give it your best! It's about everything you care for. It's about your life.

If you find a better way, does this mean that you'll have to start from zero? No. And that's exactly what makes this book and this system so powerful. You'll probably just need to remove a Skill and replace it with an upgraded version.

I want you to know that the journey won't be easy and that you won't become a superhero in the process (if you do, let me know how). If you believe that anybody is any better than you, you are wrong. All people you see on TV and magazine covers are just as weak and imperfect as you are. And they are as powerful and amazing as you are too.

You don't need to be a superhero to change the world. And you certainly don't need to be a superhero to live an incredible life. Winning is for all of us, my friend. We can all become a part of the 0.1%.

Even though I created this system myself, and I must be the best example of how it's used and how it makes you great (which it really does), I still have my ugly moments where I sleep until noon, eat junk, skip the gym, and spend most of the day in my underwear with a finger up my nose. Such days are now a very rare exception, rather than the norm, but I still have them. You will probably have some of those too, even with The Method in your hand.

Whenever that happens, don't beat yourself up. Just go back to The Method and keep doing the work. That's the beauty of the system. You don't need to always be perfect. You just need to know that you haven't performed as great as you could have and then do better, one Skill at a time.

Every Skill matters. Every little success matters. Dream big and start small. Just like you've learned to drive a car, you won't remember when you became the person you didn't believe you could ever become and when you got all the things you've always dreamed of.

My friend, it's time!

One day, life will flash before your eyes just like a movie in a theater. When that moment comes, make sure you have given your best to make this movie a masterpiece worth watching.

Remember that when this happens, you won't care about that TV show you didn't watch or about that one time you didn't go to the club. When that day comes, you will look back, and you will ask yourself:

Did I live my life or someone else's?
Did I allow myself to love and experience happiness?
Did I fully express my true, best self into the world?
Did I serve a Mission that matters?

And if you did the work, there won't be an answer that will bring anything else but pure joy to your heart. You would have lived a successful life. A fulfilled life. A life with no regret. A life in the top 0.1%.

When you give yourself the chance to experience the benefits of the system for just a couple of weeks, you will never want to go back to your old way of being.

When you look at yourself in the mirror, and you see a healthier, stronger you, when you feel the vibrancy streaming through your veins, you'll know that you are on your way to becoming the master of your Health.

When you spend time with the people you love, with your colleagues, with friends, and you notice the feeling of contentment, the gratitude, the love, the honest care, when you feel the strengthening connections between everyone, you'll know that you are becoming a master of your Relationships.

When you experience more peace, happiness, and excitement, instead of constant stress and fear, you'll know that you are becoming a master of your Emotions.

When you start following a Mission that is in alignment with your Values; when you set brave Goals, and you take focused, strategic steps toward their realization, you'll know that this is the only way you want to live for the rest of your life.

When you set your Money game to work in your favor and automate the whole process, you'll know that you've taken one of the most important decisions for your future.

When you start experiencing all the things you've been delaying for no good reason, when you give yourself Time to enjoy and celebrate life, you'll know that you are now truly complete.

From this moment on, start acting as if everything you do creates a massive difference! Because it does! Start acting as if achieving anything is possible! Because it is!

My friend, it's time!

It's time to rise up to the challenges in your life!

It's time to go out into the world and take what is yours!

You deserve every great thing you've ever dreamed of.

Are you going to play the game of life, or are you going to let the game play you?

It's time to wake up!

It's time to start your journey to greatness!

You have all that it takes!

It's all up to you now!

IT'S TIME!

ABOUT THE AUTHOR

SIMEON IVANOV is an entrepreneur, author of the 0.1%, and an ex-professional formula racing driver. After graduating, he joined his brother on a journey to build a medical company from zero to a $15M business in just five years. After selling the business in Bulgaria, Simeon moved to the United States with the goal of attempting to write the most valuable book that was ever written.

Simeon's name was on the list of the "World's Top 100 Most Popular Racing Drivers" in Driver Database 2007 classification. He was awarded "Best Racing Driver of the Year" twice in the two years he raced in his country. He won the South-East European Karting Championship twice in two attempts in his first and second racing seasons. He raced in Formula Renault 2.0 and tested in the World Series Formula Renault 3.5 in 2007, which made him one of the very few racing drivers to reach a step below F1 in just a five-year racing career.

He currently lives in Los Angeles with his family.

facebook.com/simeonivanov

instagram.com/simeonivanov